THE OLD SCHOOL

A Portrait of
Caulfield Grammar School
in 50 Lives

DAVID THOMSON

Copyright © 2019 David Thomson

Published by Connor Court Publishing

ALL RIGHTS RESERVED. This book contains material protected under International and Federal Copyright Laws and Treaties. Any unauthorised reprint or use of this material is prohibited. No part of this book may be reproduced or transmitted in any form or by any means, electronic or mechanical, including photocopying, recording, or by any information storage and retrieval system without express written permission from the publisher.

CONNOR COURT PUBLISHING PTY LTD
PO Box 7257
Redland Bay QLD 4165
sales@connorcourt.com
www.connorcourtpublishing.com.au

ISBN: 9781925826708

Cover design by Maria Giordano

The front cover cartoon by Ric Hawkins, first published in the 1964 issue of *The Caulfield Grammarian,* (used with permission).

Printed in Australia

Headmasters and Principals of Caulfield Grammar School

The Reverend J.H. Davies	1881 – 1888
The Reverend E.J. Barnett	1888 – 1896
Mr W.M. Buntine	1896 – 1932
Mr F.H.J. Archer	1923 – 1954
The Reverend Canon S.W. Kurrle, OBE	1955 – 1964
Mr B.C. Lumsden	1965 – 1977
The Reverend A.S. Holmes	1977 – 1992
Mr S.H. Newton, AO	1993 – 2011
The Reverend A.P. Syme	2011 – 2017
Mr A.R. Martin	2018 -

For Lachlan Rayner

INTRODUCTION

This is a book about the "vicissitudes of life", a phrase I heard twice in one day, first said by my friend Jeffery Barnes over coffee at La Trobe University and, second, by one of the cast of *Cosi*, the Year 10 play which I saw the same evening at Caulfield Grammar School.

The characters about whom I have written are a varied lot. Some are well known and made substantial contributions to our country. Others may not have been so successful. Some lived long lives; some died when they were young.

One led the Royal Australian Air Force while another was murdered in a lane in St Kilda and another, I hope, literally found greener pastures. One had a row with Lawrence of Arabia in Damascus and one fought the Australian Army in the High Court.

The vicissitudes in their lives brought them all, at some stage, to Caulfield, some as young pupils, some as teachers and some who were neither. All, to me, were interesting people who did interesting things. Some I knew very well, some I did not know at all. Some I taught and some taught me.

There are very few women in this book and that is simply because there were very few women connected with the school until recently. Sadly for women like Prep 4 teacher Jessie Brown and librarian "Plum" Wilkins, no detailed records of their background or their private lives exist. I adored Jessie Brown. When my father drove me to school, we used to give her a lift from Seymour Road. I would have liked to have found out enough of her life to include her in this book.

Those I have chosen to write about will tell you something of my story as well as theirs but, more importantly, the book paints a portrait of the great school which has played a role in shaping the lives of all who spent time there.

Today, the school archives are in the safe hands of Judith Gibson. Writers of future books about the school will benefit from her thorough and meticulous work.

David Thomson

July, 2019

Joseph Henry Davies

1856 – 1890

Henry Davies is first because he <u>was</u> first. Indeed. There would be no Caulfield Grammar School without him. He opened his school on 25th April, 1881, with nine boys. But let's not get carried away with the idea that he had a burning passion for schoolmastering or had a glorious vision of what the school would become over the next 138 years.

He was only in it for the money! To be fair, the money was for a higher purpose. He saw the school as a way to make enough money to allow him to go to India as a missionary. That was his real goal in life. As Horace Webber, author of the school's centenary history, put it, "It is evident that the first Headmaster of Caulfield Grammar School had no ambitions or even intention to set up a school that would last longer than suited the convenience of his own career as he wished to develop it".

Henry's family had emigrated from England to New Zealand but, in 1860, fearful of the outcome of the Maori wars, came to Australia, settling in Melbourne. Henry's father died when Henry was 12, just a year after the lad had started working in his father's solicitor's office. He was an industrious boy who matriculated at 15 and it looked like he was headed for a career in the law.

Reflecting his deeply religious upbringing, he turned his

back on the law and, at the age of 20, travelled to India where his sister, Sarah, was working with the Church Missionary Society. After two years, he returned to Australia, having failed to fit in with fellow missionaries who considered him unqualified for the work. He was also in poor health.

Commencing an arts degree at the University of Melbourne, he continued to preach, eventually travelling to many Victorian towns in the process.

With his health improved and an arts degree secured with excellent results, he announced on 26th March, 1881, that he had decided to open a school which would allow him to employ his brothers and his sister who would become the school's first matron.

On 16th April, he secured premises at the western corner of Glen Huntly Road and Selwyn Street in Elsternwick. The school opened on 25th April. In the school's centenary year, stone plaques were placed in the pavement in front of each of the school's former sites. They remained there for years until some jobsworth in the Glen Eira City Council ordered their removal "in case someone slipped on one of the plaques and was injured".

At 25, Henry became a headmaster. Over the next four years, he battled financial difficulties and outbreaks of typhoid in Caulfield but the school continued to grow.

In 1882, Henry purchased five acres of land on what is now Regent Street and he built a brick schoolroom. Returning to India would have to wait a little longer – but not forever.

In April 1888, there were 96 students enrolled of whom 32 were boarders. He had paid off the mortgage of the new site, cleared his debts and had set aside £1,000 for Mary and a similar amount to get him to India. He had also found a young Anglican clergyman who was showing interest in taking over the school. He was the Reverend Ernest Barnett.

Henry left the school on 24th August and he began to put in place his plan to go to India with the Church Missionary Society. Arrangements for his ordination were almost completed when he discovered that the Anglicans would only ordain him as a priest after he had served six months as a deacon. In Henry's view, that was a waste of six months.

He discovered that he could be ordained by the Presbyterian Church so he took himself off to Edinburgh via the Holy Land for a course in theology. Returning to Melbourne in May 1889, he was ordained at The Scots' Church in Collins Street, on 5th August. He and Mary sailed for Hong Kong on 20th August and he arrived in Seoul shortly afterwards to join the American Presbyterian Mission. He spent some months learning the language and headed for Pusan on 16th March, 1890. He was the first Australian missionary in Korea.

Unfortunately, Henry and Mary had failed to be vaccinated against smallpox and Henry became ill. He reached Pusan on 6th April and died the following day. He was buried on a hillside overlooking the town. A headstone was erected but it has long since disappeared.

Such is the regard for Henry, theology students from Korea

regularly visit Caulfield to see the school he set up to allow him to become a missionary.

Edward Daley

1901-1985

Ted Daley was born on 23rd January 1901 at Bendigo in country Victoria where his father was a school teacher. In 1915, he arrived at Caulfield Grammar School. When I interviewed him in the early 1980s about his schooldays, he recalled Frank Archer as a friendly and generous-minded master who taught the boys a great deal about living. Of R.W. McCulloch, he recalled an immense teaching capacity in his areas of physics and he remembered Arthur Astley as a grand old man, a gentleman and a fine influence on those who were in his classes. I noted that he did not mention W.S. Morcom, one of the icons of the era. When pressed, Ted grimaced and offered his assessment: "He was a dreadful bully!" He must have fallen foul of "The Claw" somewhere along the line.

The school records suggest that Ted was a very capable pupil although he claimed that it was sheer hard work which gained him honours in matriculation physics in 1919. He was a very good tennis player and represented the school in the First IV.

After studying at the University of Melbourne where he graduated in medicine in 1925, he worked at Warrnambool and at the Austin Hospital in Melbourne, then spent a further two years in private practice. At The Scots' Church, Melbourne, on 21st July 1927 he married Katharine Grace Wright-Smith. On 16 July 1928, he joined the Royal Australian Air Force as a Flight Lieutenant. One of only three doctors in the permanent Air Force, he served at Laverton and Point Cook. In 1930 he took the unusual step of qualifying as a pilot to improve his ability to assess candidates for flying training, and to estimate flying fatigue. He was promoted to Squadron Leader in November 1933. In 1936 he went to England on exchange.

Believing that any coming war would involve action in the tropics, Ted completed a Diploma in Tropical Medicine at the University of Liverpool. He enjoyed his two years in England and gained considerable insight into Royal Air Force medical administration. When he returned to Australia in July 1938, he was appointed Deputy-Director (Director from January 1939) of Medical Services with the rank of Wing Commander. He immediately introduced RAF methods of organisation and documentation, which proved invaluable after the outbreak of World War II and allowed RAF and RAAF medical units to operate together with precision.

In June 1940, Ted was promoted to temporary Group Captain. That year he initiated the building of No.1 RAAF Hospital, Laverton, where intensive training of medical staff took place. He introduced No.1 Air Ambulance Unit to the Middle East in 1941. He was appointed honorary physician to King George VI in 1942 (and later to Queen Elizabeth II) and was elected a fellow of the Royal Australasian College of Physicians in 1943. In July 1944, on D-Day +32, he took the brave step of visiting Normandy to observe the British practice of flying casualties home rather than setting up hospitals in France.

Promoted to acting Air Commodore in August 1945, Ted was made Director-General of Medical Services in December. He rose to Air Vice-Marshal in March 1952 and that year was appointed a Commander of the Order of the British Empire. In 1956 he formed the RAAF School of Aviation Medicine at Point Cook and served on the medical committee for the Melbourne Olympic Games. He had established the special group on aviation medicine of the British Medical Association in Australia in 1949 and was its first chairman. In 1954 he was elected a vice-president of the Aeronautical Medical Association of the United States of America when he attended the 25th anniversary congress of the association in Washington at the invitation of the Surgeon-General of the United States Air Force. He delivered an address at the congress and spent some weeks inspecting medical establishments and research work in the USA and Canada.

Ted retired from the RAAF on 31 March 1961. Recognised as an outstanding administrator, he became national director of the St John Ambulance Association from 1961 to 1975. He supervised the rewriting of the first-aid manual to reflect Australian conditions and was appointed in 1962 a Knight of Grace of the Order of St John of Jerusalem. From 1965 to 1968 he was president of the Victorian section of the Royal

Flying Doctor Service of Australia.

Though initially seeming austere, with a piercing gaze and toothbrush moustache, one soon discovered that he was a kind and gentle man with a keen sense of humour and a love of music and tennis. He died on 15th March 1985 in his home at East Malvern. His body was bequeathed to the Department of Anatomy at the University of Melbourne.

Robert Fowler

1888 – 1965

In 2015, the Royal Australasian College of Surgeons held an exhibition in Melbourne entitled "Anzac Surgeons of Gallipoli". One of the surgeons commemorated in the exhibition was Robert Fowler.

Robert was born in East Smithfield in London and his family immigrated to Australia when Robert was three years-old. The family first settled in Echuca and later in Bendigo and Robert came to Caulfield as a boarder in 1900 to finish his secondary education.

By 1909, he had completed Bachelor of Medicine and Bachelor of Surgery degrees at the University of Melbourne and gained a Doctor of Medicine degree in 1912. On the way to his doctorate, he was named Beaney Scholar in pathology in 1911 and in the following hear he assisted in lectures in that subject.

After completing his initial degrees, Robert joined the Citizen Military Forces. Within three weeks of the start of the Great War, he was appointed a Captain in the Australian Army Medical Corps and, two months later, was dispatched to Egypt where he commanded the 1st Light Horse Field Ambulance. There he was based but much of his time was spent working in hospital ships evacuating wounded from Gallipoli. His war diary paints a vivid picture: "14 June 1915 2.45 am landed at Anzac Cove off lighter . . . slept on the beach near a stack of biscuit tins until awakened at daybreak by shrapnel . . . The shells then found their way to the gully next to ours and we were free except for their screeching overhead".

Following the carefully orchestrated evacuation of Gallipoli, extraordinarily without the loss of a single life, four divisions of Australians were shipped to France between March and June 1916, while the mounted Australians under Major-General Chauvel remained to defend Egypt.

In February 1917, Robert, now a Colonel, commanded the 4th Light Horse Field Ambulance in the advance through Palestine, arriving in Damascus in October. Robert found the population in a terrible state from malaria, dysentery, thirst and starvation. It was here that he met Colonel T.E. Lawrence, "Lawrence of Arabia" as he would soon be known. Lawrence wrote a somewhat dramatic version of their meeting in his book *Seven Pillars of Wisdom* which was repeated in David Lean's 1962 film *Lawrence of Arabia*. Robert insisted that at no point did he slap Lawrence across the face.

The two men discussed the terrible state of the Turkish hospital. Lawrence visited the building, in reality converted barracks, and was appalled by what he saw. With little co-operation from the British authorities, Lawrence galvanised the prisoners into action. He fed them, gave them tools, the dead were buried and the building disinfected.

In 1919, Robert was appointed an Officer of the Order of the British Empire. During the war, he had been Mentioned in Dispatches on three separate occasions.

Returning to Australia in 1920, he continued his work as a surgeon whilst remaining a member of the citizen forces.

Like Ted Daley, Robert had an interest in the potential for patients to be evacuated and the military importance of tropical medicine to Australia. Appointed a Group Captain in the RAAF, he commanded the 117th Australian General Hospital in Toowoomba, Queensland, from 1942 to 1943 and was appointed Deputy Director of Medical Services from 1943 to 1944.

Robert had been appointed a Fellow of the Royal College of Surgeons in England in 1920, the American College of Surgeons in 1924, and the Royal Australian College of Surgeons in 1927.

As early as 1921, Robert was Honorary Obstetric Surgeon at the Women's Hospital and later Honorary Gynaecologist at the Alfred Hospital where he contributed to the treatment of uterine cancer. In 1955, his research asserted "the positive association of lung cancer and tobacco smoking". The Anti-

Cancer Council of Victoria established an annual travelling scholarship in his name.

Throughout his life, Robert maintained close links with the University of Melbourne, being a member of the standing committee of convocation from 1932, warden in 1959 and a council member in 1962.

Bill Callander

1929 – 2013

Bill was educated at The Geelong College and the University of Sydney where he completed a Bachelor of Arts degree and Diploma in Education. He had given some thought to becoming a Presbyterian minister but the classroom began to appeal more than the pulpit. He taught for five years at Newington College in Sydney before coming to Caulfield as Senior English Master in 1957.

Soon making his mark as an outstanding classroom teacher, Bill ably led the English staff and broke ground teaching modern texts and handling the classics with flair, engaging students equally with Golding and Chaucer. Working with Norman Kaye and Tony Kitton, Bill contributed substantially to the writing of the musical *Bullumbimbi*, directed by Bill Sayers and performed in the new Memorial Hall in 1958.

The Theatre Guild, cadets, student publications, debating and Thursday activities all felt Bill's positive guidance. In fact, there were few aspects of life in the school that he did not influence. He was instrumental in developing the summer schools held in the early 1960s and assisted Stan Kurrle and Bruce Lumsden in streamlining the administration of the school at all levels. Such was his interest in school administration that he became one of the early students in the Diploma of Educational Administration course at the University of New England, completing the course in 1969.

Stan Kurrle appointed Bill as Deputy Chief of Staff in 1962 and Senior Master in 1963. In 1968, Bill spent Term 3 on exchange at Nelson College, the oldest boys' state school in New Zealand. On his return, he amused the Caulfield staff by telling them that the Nelson Common Room had a telephone hotline to the bar at the local staff "watering hole" in case a staff member were needed back at school in a hurry.

Headmaster Bruce Lumsden appointed him Deputy Headmaster in 1971. It was almost being handed a poisoned chalice at a time when society at large was in turmoil and students were more inclined to be rebellious than at any time before or since but Bill managed to get even some of the most difficult students on side by the sheer force of his personality.

Unfortunately, Bill's private life was not quite so successful. One detractor described him as a "serial husband" which was not entirely inaccurate. His first marriage, to Joyce with whom he had five children, ended in divorce when he began a relationship with a young art teacher. This led to Bill getting the cold shoulder from the wives of some of his colleagues. That marriage also ended in divorce.

Bill introduced Film Study at Year 11 and developed a wide reading scheme, both programs later copied by other schools. He developed a General Language course for Year 7 students, writing his own materials. He organized staff seminars which led to significant developments in curriculum and he strongly promoted the outdoor education program at Yarra Junction. The School Committee was another of the innovations which came about in Bill's time as Deputy Headmaster. They were a group of leaders elected by the students who replaced the system of prefects appointed by the headmaster.

On 12th January 1970, while still at Caulfield, Bill was appointed principal-elect of the Education Reform Association School to be opened at Donvale in 1971. In an extensive article written for *The Age*, he set out his plans for this revolutionary school which was to be built in a bush setting with a forest study area, theatre, café, open-air science laboratory and a sheltered grove for music students. He explained his role as taking the student at the age of 12 or so and helping him become more fully and completely himself, while recognizing that parents play the main part in bringing up their children and having a decisive influence upon their attitudes and habits, the way they act and the way they see life.

In the article, Bill set out the type of teachers he would employ. They must have the training, the knowledge, the zest and imagination, and the human understanding to set off, control and guide the educating process. He made it clear that his school would have no room for the petty dictator, nor for the weak, the cynical or the humourless. His teachers would have to have sufficient confidence to give children wide margins of freedom and self-determination but must also have the strength to provide a sound framework of law and order within which the students would feel safe.

He wanted flexibility in his school: flexible timetables, flexible walls, flexible furniture, flexible grounds. Flexible walls would allow students to avoid being locked into fixed classes of 30 or 40 which would diminish their being treated as individuals. Flexible timetables would allow for different children to be learning at different rates. Bill planned to ensure that students would have a wide range of learning experiences rather than be confined by rigid sets of subjects. Students would have a say in setting the curriculum and there would be no examinations, except for the public Matriculation requirements.

He gave me a copy of the splendid brochure which had been printed to market the school, complete with photographs by Don Wirth. I told him that I thought it was an excellent production. He smiled and pointed to a photograph of an angelic-looking boy with a guinea pig on his shoulder, seemingly doing his homework. Bill said, "Turn it upside down and see what he is writing". I did and we both burst out laughing. The boy was writing verses of *The Good Ship Venus*, a particularly vulgar piece of verse. I treasure my copy!

Despite his involvement in all the planning for the school, contractual difficulties made him decide not to take up the appointment as headmaster. As it turned out, it was a fortuitous decision. The school opened in 1971 and, over the next 16 years, seven principals came and went. By 1986, only one student reached Higher School Certificate level and the school closed in 1987.

In his report at the end of the year, Caulfield's Headmaster, Bruce Lumsden, paid his tribute to Bill: "Mr Callander, the Deputy Headmaster, has come to the belief that, after 17 years' service at Caulfield, he should venture out into new fields. I well understand his thoughts, but have more reason than most to appreciate how much he will be missed. He has brought particular gifts of mind and judgement to the school and has exercised very significant influence on important aspects of the spirit and work of the school. My personal debt to him for his advice, his constructive thinking, his willing sharing of responsibility and his loyalty is very great".

Farewelled from Caulfield at the end of 1973 following a grand dinner at The Gables in Malvern, Bill joined the Commonwealth's education service and became Principal of Casuarina High School in Darwin from 1974 to 1977. At the end of 1974, Cyclone Tracy devastated Darwin and Casuarina High School virtually became the "Northern Suburbs Area School" and comprised a crèche, pre-school, primary and high school in one, while the surrounding schools were rebuilt. The school population at the time rose up to 1200. By 1976 the school was back to normal operations and a Music

School was established on the site. In 1977 an Agricultural Science program was established.

Such was the outstanding work done by Bill in Darwin, he was appointed founding principal of Copland College in Canberra in 1978 and he remained in that role until 1983.

He returned to Melbourne in 1984 as Deputy Principal of International House in the University of Melbourne and married a third time, which was also not to last.

In retirement, Bill undertook archival research for the Berry Street organization and occasionally assisted in the archives at Caulfield. For a time, he lived on a rural property at Linton, north of Melbourne, and then moved to Buderim in Queensland where he remained until his death in 2013.

In his own words, Bill had enduring "concern for the growth of good and happy people". He exercised that concern for the benefit of the thousands of students in his care over many years. He was, quite simply, a perfect teacher.

Trevor Pyman

1916 – 1995

Trevor Ashmore Pyman was born in Melbourne on Christmas Day 1916 and grew up in Caulfield, not far from the school at which he commenced in 1924 at the age of eight.

By 1926, he had been elected Form Captain and captain of his form's football team as well as Secretary of the Third Form Corner, a writing club which produced a form newspaper, the Third Form Star.

Over the next five years, Trevor was regularly elected vice-captain of his form, achieved high academic results and developed his cricket and football skills.

In 1932, he passed Intermediate and was selected as a bowler in the First XI. The following year, he became a member of the School House Committee and was appointed a Probationer Prefect. He took part in a range of house activities and was duly awarded House Colours.

His final year at Caulfield, 1934, saw him as a Prefect, Vice-Captain of the School and on stage playing the lead in "Leave it to Psmith" performed at the Caulfield Town Hall on 21st July. He was also a member of the school debating team, played First XI cricket and First XVIII football – initially playing forward but later, more successfully, on the backline. He rounded off an outstanding year as Dux of School and headed to the University of Melbourne.

In his own words, Caulfield "was a happy school society. Relations between pupils and staff were generally harmonious and on a basis of mutual respect and co-operation. Some teachers were particularly noted for their ability to communicate and even win extraordinary respect and popularity. 'Smithy' (Gemmell Lamb Smith) was an outstanding example of this attitude – he won great respect in his endeavour to promote hobbies and crafts. I have no doubt he had a substantial influence with boys who needed guidance and practical advice and who hovered on the brink of serious misconduct".

Studying history and political science, Trevor graduated with a Bachelor of Arts degree with honours in 1938, the same year in which he was elected to the committee of the Caulfield Grammarians' Association. In 1940, he graduated Bachelor of Laws with honours and undertook articles with the firm of Hedderwick Fookes and Alston. That firm merged with Arthur Robinson & Co. in 1984 and two of Trevor's sons were partners in that merged firm, which gave their father much satisfaction.

By then, World War Two had started so Trevor attempted to join the Royal Australian Air Force but was rejected because of an issue with his eyesight. Not to be put off military service, he joined the Melbourne University Rifles under National Service provisions and was assigned to Headquarters Home Forces under the command of Lieutenant-General Iven Mackay.

For one so well qualified, it must have been frustrating to have been kept in relatively trivial work as a clerk. He was gradually promoted, to corporal then to sergeant and eventually commissioned as a lieutenant in the Army Education Service in 1943. At last he felt as if he were doing something that was appropriate to his abilities and that was of some help to his fellow servicemen.

Against the background of war, Trevor continued his studies. He had been admitted to practise by the Supreme Court in

1941. On 1st August 1942, he married Margaret Haddon Hall at St Mary's, Caulfield, settling in Alston Grove in Balaclava. Released from war service in October 1944, he joined the Australian diplomatic service and added to his qualifications a Master of Laws degree in 1945 and a Diploma in Public Administration in 1946.

Before the war, Trevor had been unable to choose between a life in a legal profession, for which he was formally qualified, or in the field of international relations through employment in the Department of External Affairs. As it happened, he applied for a position in the Department which had been advertised in the press. He wrote out his application in an army transit camp in Brisbane on his way back to Mount Isa in mid-1944. Several months later, he was advised that his application had been successful.

There began a 14-year career in the diplomatic service which included his appointment as Acting High Commissioner to Canada in 1954-57 and Head of Chancery and Counsellor at the Australian Embassy in Washington in 1957-58 which included membership of the Australian Delegation at the General Assembly of the United Nations.

By 1958, Trevor and Margaret had made the decision that their children would not be sent to boarding schools for their education. This led to Trevor resigning from the Department of External Affairs and returning to Melbourne to live. He spent a short time with the Federal Department of Labour before joining the Department of Civil Aviation, becoming head of the International Relations group within the Department. Prior to his retirement from the Department at the end of 1977, he served for some years as a Commonwealth Government representative on the board of Australian National Airlines.

Retirement from the public service did not mean that Trevor gave up work altogether. He became a consultant in the Faculty of Law at Monash University where he was also Senior Lecturer in International and Australian Aviation Law and where he not only played a significant role in the development of the technical knowledge of the law by several generations of students, but encouraged in them a wisdom, an integrity and a compassion in the application of the law.

Trevor was the middle of three brothers who all attended Caulfield in the 1920s and 1930s. His older brother, Clive, became a well-known ear nose and throat surgeon; his younger brother, Jim, School Captain in 1940 and Captain of the First XI, became a respected pharmacist. Trevor often downgraded his own achievements by saying that he was just one of many high achievers of that generation.

Trevor died on 2nd April 1995. A private family funeral on 6th April was followed later that day by a service of thanksgiving at St Mary's Church, Caulfield. The church was packed.

The Trevor Pyman Prize for Legal Studies was introduced in 2015 and is awarded to the top student in Legal Studies at Caulfield Campus and Wheelers Hill Campus. It commemorates Trevor's contribution to Australia's role in international affairs.

Michael Hanley

1925 – 2000

No-one could have foreseen what lay ahead for Michael Hanley when he left the staff of Caulfield Grammar School at the end of 1962.

Michael was one of the "bright young things" Headmaster Stan Kurrle employed to improve the standard of education offered at the school. Appointed to the English staff under Bill Callander, Michael joined Davies House and became Form Master of IIIQ, the Year 9 high-achievers class. Capitalising on Michael's athletic background, Stan also appointed him Master-in-Charge of Athletics and the lift in the boys' performances by the end of the year was noticeable.

Born in South Africa, the son of an Anglican clergyman, Michael looked like he was heading for a short life. When only a few months old, he managed to elude his nanny and crawled into the town's open drainage system. Loud barking of the family dog at a sluice gate resulted in Michael's rescue. At eight, perched on the handlebars of his bicycle, which was being driven by a friend, resulted in a crash in which Michael's skull was fractured. This led to a slight weakness in his vision and on his left side. Despite this, he went on to academic and sporting success at St Andrew's College, in what is now Makhanda, where he excelled in rugby and athletics and was captain of his house.

The year after he arrived at Caulfield, Michael became an officer in the cadet unit. The ribbons on his uniform jacket revealed that he had served in the Second World War, seeing service with the field artillery unit of the 6th South African Armoured Division in Egypt and in Italy.

After the war, Michael enrolled at Rhodes University where he completed a Bachelor of Arts degree, seeming to fit his study around a plethora of sports. He captained his college in athletics and the Eastern Province team at the South African Championships in 1949.

Michael joined the staff of Queen's College in 1950 and, whilst on leave in London in 1954, met Australian-born Claire Rosier. They were married in 1955. A short-lived career change took place in 1956 when Michael worked for Prudential Insurance, a post he held for two years.

After their third child was born, Michael and Claire moved to Australia. They sensed that the social and political situation in South Africa would not allow the kind of life they wanted for themselves and their children. They settled in South Caulfield and Michael began teaching at Caulfield at the beginning of 1959.

Michael's impact on Caulfield was immediate. He demonstrated great skill as a teacher and coach of athletics and 2nd XI cricket. He was promoted to Captain in the cadet unit in 1961 as a company commander and training officer. In 1962, the athletics team was placed third in the Associated Public Schools' Combined Sports, the highest position it had ever held. He also managed to find time to complete a Bachelor of Education degree.

In the second half of 1962, Michael discovered that Geelong Grammar School was seeking a replacement for the founding head of its Timbertop campus near Mansfield. He took up the post at the start of 1963. He and Claire took to the place with relish and the staff and boys took to them both. The relative calm of Timbertop looked as if it might be shattered when it was announced that the Prince of Wales, then almost 17, would come to Timbertop on exchange from his school, Gordonstoun, in Scotland, for a term in 1966. As it turned out, Michael handled the visit very successfully. The Prince chose to stay for an extra term and later said that his time there was the happiest of his schooldays, a statement he has made on a number of occasions since. That was in no small measure due to Michael's ability to handle every aspect of those two terms which the school would not normally have had to experience.

Michael left Timbertop in 1968 and taught geography and English at Corio and assisted in the administration of the school for the next 15 years. In 1982, Michael and Claire retired to their house at Airey's Inlet.

The value of Michael's contributions to Caulfield and to Geelong cannot be over-estimated. Those who were lucky enough to be in his classes or out in the bush with him at Yarra Junction or at Timbertop would agree that the "chalky" from South Africa with the mop of grey hair was well worth knowing.

Claire Crocker

1919 – 2000

Claire Crocker was a member of staff for only a short time but she proved to be a very interesting member of the Common Room and exceptionally good company.

Born in Queensland, Claire moved with her family to Perth in 1922 as her father, John Frederick Ward, had been appointed the founding Headmaster of Wesley College. They moved again in 1929 when Ward became Headmaster of Prince Alfred College in Adelaide. Claire was educated at Methodist Ladies' College and then studied economics and English at Adelaide University but left after one year. Learning typing and shorthand and other secretarial skills, she worked for two years as her father's secretary at the school.

In the 1940s, Claire married Dr John Gooden, a brilliant physicist, and went with him to Birmingham where he worked on atomic physics with Mark Oliphant. Unfortunately, John developed nephritis so Claire brought him and their two year-old adopted son home to Australia where John died in 1950.

While they had been in Birmingham, John Gooden and Mark Oliphant and their wives became good friends. About the time of John's death, Oliphant was appointed to a senior post at the Australian National University in Canberra. He gave Claire a job as his secretary.

Also working at ANU was Walter Crocker, Professor of

International Relations. Claire fell in love with the engaging South Australian and a new life opened up for her after their marriage. In 1952, Claire gave birth to a son and Walter was appointed Australia's High Commissioner to India. The Crockers moved to Indonesia in 1955, the so-called "year of living dangerously" because of the attempted coup by the "30th September Movement". Three years later they were in Canada and from 1958 to 1962 they returned to India. At the same time, Walter was also Ambassador to Nepal. From 1963 to 1965 they were in the Netherlands and Belgium.

By this time, it had become clear that Claire and Walter were no longer compatible and their marriage was dissolved in 1958.

For the next decade, Claire concentrated on looking after her adolescent sons then, in 1976, she changed direction again and became Matron of Manifold House at Geelong Grammar School where she served with distinction for six years.

In the 1981 issue of *The Corian*, Claire's Housemaster, Paul Sheahan, wrote that "she brought all the qualities of an ambassadress and the common sense of a mother to her duties here. Band-Aids and liniments were dispensed with never a terse word but, just as frequently, it was her friendly ear and sound advice that boys craved".

In 1981, Claire moved to Melbourne and joined the staff at Caulfield where she was surrogate mother to 90 boarders. In the day school, she looked after the infirmary, ministering to the needs of boys who benefited from her calm understanding of just about anything that befell them.

After retiring from Caulfield, Claire divided her time between family and friends, writing short stories, painting delicate watercolours of flowers and finishing her novel *Peacocks Dancing* which was published after her death.

A trait we all recognized was her unconditional friendship. She enjoyed visiting the Common Room, especially for Friday drinks, where colleagues enjoyed her wide-ranging conversations. Her son, Robert, once wrote of her "insight into the ultimate emptiness of wealth and social privilege and power" and her clear understanding "that God's love respects no conventional formulas or traditional prejudices". The school was poorer for her leaving.

Kenneth Barrett

1934 – 2014

Ken, as he was universally known, was a student at Caulfield from 1943 to 1952. He was a keen reader and joined the senior library committee, becoming School Officer for the library when he was in Year 12. His real passion, however, was theatre. His mother delighted in taking him to live shows and to the cinema and encouraged him to take part in school productions.

In 1953, Ken began studying English and history at the

University of Melbourne, completing a Bachelor of Arts degree and a Diploma in Education and participating in university revues. He returned to Caulfield as a resident master in the boarding house, then known as School House, in 1957 while he was studying at the university. In 1959, he began full-time teaching and involved himself in a wide range of school activities.

In 1961, he travelled to England where he taught at Fernden School at Haslemere in Surrey where he coached the cricket team and also played for the local village team. He returned to Caulfield in 1962.

Throughout his working life, Ken demonstrated an extraordinary versatility. His first teaching role at Caulfield was as a form master of Year 7 where he taught a variety of subjects but it was not long before he became head of the History Department. As a member of his old house, he became Year 10 Buntine group teacher, responsible for administrative matters and pastoral care. He would become Housemaster of Buntine in 1967. He also gave much to the development of activities at the school's outdoor education centre at Yarra Junction, especially in the early years.

A competent schoolboy cricketer, Ken went on to play with the Caulfield Grammarians Association team and then coached at Caulfield, eventually in 1979 the Second XI. In the years that followed, Ken variously coached Australian Rules football, became Master-in-Charge of soccer and was a high-jump coach with the school's athletics squad.

Ken's interest in theatre led to his involvement in the

production of many school plays and he directed the annual school revue, a highlight throughout the 1970s.

A student newspaper, *demos*, was launched in 1965 under Ken's leadership and was published until 1978. In 1967, Ken initiated the publication of *Extempore*, a literary magazine containing students' original writing and photographs. It launched the careers of a number of writers and continued as an annual publication until recently.

Ken played a significant part in the annual Theatre Guild Service Week Tours which took student performers of all sorts to Tally Ho Boys' Home, Burwood House and aged care homes from North Melbourne to Camberwell and parts beyond. There were musical items, a short play or two, a ventriloquist and sundry sketches. But not all the drama occurred on stage. None will forget the minor collision between Ken's Volkswagen and the elderly van carrying the stage equipment or a rather grand Armstrong Siddeley descending the Burke Road hill with its rather dodgy cable brakes playing up – but there were no real disasters.

He joined a number of colleagues to write the curriculum for a new subject, human relations, in 1970. At the time, it was unique and, over the next decade, it paved the way for subjects taught today such as health and human relations and sociology. He had been an active member of the Common Room, serving as President of the Staff Association on two occasions. In this capacity, he provided strong leadership and secured improvements in staff welfare.

Ken was an engaging teacher and coach who developed close

relationships with students and their families. This did not sit well with some of his more conservative colleagues who drip-fed baseless gossip and innuendo to the Headmaster who terminated Ken's employment at the end of 1982. He was advised to take legal action for unfair dismissal but refused to be involved in litigation with the school he loved.

A post at Trinity Grammar School was being advertised. Ken applied and was snapped up to teach history and English. His appointment was no doubt helped by the excellent support he received from Caulfield's Senior Master, John Nelson, who said in his reference, "The dedication and professional manner in which Ken has pursued his career has earned him permanent recognition in this school. I believe he is among the most creative, influential and successful teachers I have encountered in my 21 years of teaching".

At Trinity as at Caulfield, he demonstrated his versatility, taking on the additional roles of integrated studies co-ordinator, coach of the cricket Second XI and introducing, in 1984, the annual *Trinity Revue*. It was through the revue that Ken was to make an extraordinary impact by opening drama to a large number of boys and developing the writing, acting and production skills of many. Trinity old boys still talk of his first sketch *Laughing Les* which was based on Les Hocking, the Deputy Headmaster, renowned for his serious, somewhat severe approach to schoolmastering. They were fearful that their skit might incur his wrath. It was a gamble that paid off as May, Les's wife, laughed so loudly that the rest of the audience were caught in the humorous slipstream

In 1989, Ken took over as Head of Drama. Central to Ken's approach was the belief that literature and literacy could be gained through acting and staging. In 2003, Trinity's centenary year, Ken held his 52nd production, *Wholly Trinity, The Centenary Stage Show*, a combination of literature and history in dialogue, dance, song and archival film footage. Ken's centenary history of drama at Trinity, *Play On!*, is an eloquent statement of his commitment to theatre and its place in education.

Ken retired at the end of 2003. He maintained links with both of "his schools". Many of his former students participated in his memorial service in 2014 which included a series of amazing and amusing sketches which Ken would have loved. He was sent off in style.

John McNutt

1879-1971

Notes for an article written by the school's fourth headmaster, Frank Archer, listed significant positions held by former students of Caulfield Grammar School. Archer wrote that one was headmaster of an English public school. As no names were mentioned in the notes, some detective work was necessary. A search through documents held in the school archives revealed the name: John Stuart Macnutt, Headmaster of Canford School in Dorset and, later, of Seaford College in Sussex.

John was born on 6th May, 1879, in Barnet, Hertfordshire. When John was nine, his family spent some time in the United States of America, arriving in New York on 4th June, 1888. They sailed in the *Mariposa* from San Francisco to Sydney, arriving on 2nd April 1889, and then travelled to Melbourne. Dr George Macnutt, Canadian born clergyman and surgeon, and his wife, Isabella, had nine children of whom John was the second youngest.

Initially, the family lived in the city at the corner of Flinders and Spring Streets and the four boys attended Scotch College, then nearby in East Melbourne, from June 1889 to December 1890. By 1891, Dr Macnutt had moved his family to Elsternwick and the two younger boys, Ernest and John, came to Caulfield Grammar School.

Apart from enrolment details, there is little known of many students of that time. Neither Ernest nor John seems to have won prizes but their eldest brother, Frederick, then 17, was baptised at St Mary's Church, Caulfield, on 5th September, 1891. Frederick was a member of the organizing committee and acted as timekeeper at the Annual Athletic Sports on 21st October 1892. We do not know exactly when the boys left Caulfield but it appears the whole family returned to England in 1894.

John graduated Bachelor of Arts at Trinity College, Dublin, in 1911 and Master of Arts in 1914. He became Vice-Principal of Clarence School at Weston-super-Mare. Two years later, he was appointed Principal and remained in that post until he became founding Principal of Canford School, which absorbed Clarence School, in 1923. He had been ordained a deacon in the Church of England in 1915 and a priest in 1918, serving as curate of Holy Trinity Church, Weston-super-Mare from 1915 to 1923.

Like his father, John was a world traveller at a time when it was a rare activity. Just prior to taking up his post at Canford, he had sailed to Canada in the *Londonderry* to visit his sister, Isabella, who lived in Toronto.

By 1928, the pressure of two successive headmasterships and the founding of a new school was taking its toll. He had led Clarence School, a small school of 200 boys, through the Great War with all the difficulties and strain that involved. Canford was a much bigger school and demands on the headmaster unrelenting. Advised by his doctors to take a complete break, John sailed for Australia in February 1928. Copies of *The Caulfield Grammarian* for that year show no record of his having visited his old school although visits by other clergy are mentioned.

The governors of Canford School were also responsible for Seaford College in Sussex, a small school of just 90 boys in 1928 (over 600 boys and girls in 2018) and the position of headmaster was offered to John. This appointment had been made prior to his departure from Canford and he took up his new post immediately on return from Australia.

John remained at Seaford until 1931 when, at 52, he decided he had had enough of headmastering and "retired" to the less pressurised role of Rector of Everleigh in Wiltshire. He was also Honorary Chaplain to the Bishop of Sarum from 1936 to 1946 and Rural Dean of Pewsey from 1951 to 1954.

One can only imagine the conversations which might have taken place when John dined with two of his brothers. His eldest brother, Frederick, had a distinguished career as a Church of England clergyman, becoming Archdeacon and Provost of Leicester, Chaplain to the King and a distinguished author. Another older brother, Charles, also became a Church of England priest.

By 1965, John had returned to Weston-super-Mare near Canford School where he remained until his death in 1971 at the age of 92.

Edward Honey

1885 – 1922

Do you know who first suggested silence at 11 o'clock on the 11th November to remember the dead of the Great War?

If you answered Edward Honey, you either were a pupil at Caulfield Grammar School in the last few years or you are heavily into military history. For the best part of a century, most people were completely unaware of the identity of the man whose suggestion created an "instant tradition".

Edward was born in St Kilda and came to Caulfield Grammar School in 1895. Student records of the time are very sketchy so there is little information about his involvement in school life.

On leaving school, he worked for some time in magazine publication and distribution which took him to outback Australia where he found relief from the city rush and discovered the impressiveness of stillness as a means to pause, think and remember. He travelled to New Zealand where he studied journalism and then found work in London. In 1915, he joined the British Army and served with the Middlesex Regiment although his service was cut short by ill health. Being discharged as medically unfit, he returned to journalism in London. Edward was considered a first-rate journalist. Lord Northcliffe, proprietor of the *Daily Mirror* and *The Times*, knew him and wanted to nominate him as a war correspondent but that did not eventuate.

As the war drew on, Edward observed the continuing line of injured and broken servicemen returning from various theatres of war and was deeply affected by what he saw.

As the first anniversary of the armistice approached, Edward could not forget the high spirits he witnessed on the night of 11th November, 1918. He felt that such unrestrained celebration failed to pay tribute to the horror of the past four years. He believed there should be some way of recognizing the silent grief so many of the bereaved were unable to express.

Until a few days before the anniversary of the armistice, there had been no announcement of any official plans but there had been plenty of suggestions of parades, balls and parties.

Well aware of the power of the press, Edward wrote to the London *Evening News* asking, "Can we not spare some fragment of these hours of peace and rejoicing for a silent tribute to these mighty dead? Individually yes! Too many of us know we will for our own kith and kin, for the friend who will never come back. But nationally? I would ask for five minutes, five little minutes only. Five silent minutes of national remembrance. A very sacred intercession."

Well, for a while the press did not seem all that powerful as nothing official seemed to be happening but Edward's letter had been read by someone who was prepared and able to take his suggestion further. A prominent and influential South African, Sir Percy FitzPatrick, author of the classic children's book *Jock of the Bushveld*, was impressed by Edward's idea of silence for remembrance and told Prime Minister Lloyd George who raised it with the King. His Majesty felt that silence for five minutes was impractical, even three minutes, but he accepted two minutes and, as such, it was proclaimed on 7th November. The observation of silence took place four days later and has been observed every year since in many parts of the world to remember the dead of all wars.

One might have thought that Edward may have gained celebrity status but it was not to be. He was largely forgotten and, when he died in 1922, he was buried in the Northwood Cemetery in London where his grave remains unmarked. The Imperial War Museum holds no image of him nor does the Australian War Memorial. A conversation in early 2014 with Major-General David McLachlan, then Victorian President of the RSL, sparked a search. David thought there was a photograph of Edward in the archives of his organization. He was right and a copy is now in Caulfield's archives.

On 7th May 1965, 46 years after Edward's letter to the Evening News, Melbourne's Lord Mayor, Sir Leo Curtis, unveiled a memorial plaque which had been placed on a large rock near Melbourne's Shrine of Remembrance. It bears the words "In memory of Edward George Honey who died in 1922, a Melbourne journalist who while living in London first suggested the solemn ceremony of silence."

The plaque faces the road, away from what is now a jogging path, and is largely ignored except at 10 o'clock on the morning of 11th November when a small group of Australian Defence Force personnel, a representative of Caulfield Grammar School and officials of the Shrine of Remembrance gather for a brief ceremony and place poppies on the plaque. But Edward's real and enduring memorial is the silence which takes place less than an hour later.

Glendon Lean

1944 – 1995

When Malvern Memorial Grammar School amalgamated with Caulfield Grammar School, the senior Malvern boys came to Caulfield in 1961. Many stood out as they were permitted to continue wearing their Malvern uniform. If you had not been a Malvern boy at the time or had not been at

Caulfield in 1961, you would have missed the phenomenon that was Glen Lean.

At Malvern, Glen had been a star schoolboy almost since he arrived in 1956. He had been a member of the athletics team since 1958 and was the Under 16 Athletics Champion in 1959 and captained the athletics team. In the same year, he won a Speech Night prize for academic excellence.

In 1960, Glen was appointed a prefect and Captain of Langford House. He was also assistant producer and stage manager for the school production of *Toad of Toad Hall*.

The editor of the final issue of *The Malvern Grammarian* described him thus – with an allusion to Shakespeare: "Glen Lean – and with a hungry look; a super-scientist with pedagogical leanings; abhors the proletariat; is attracted by things theatrical and is constantly playing a schizophrenic game of hide-and-seek between the characters of Hamlet and Auntie Mame".

Somewhat eclipsed by the well-established stars of Caulfield's Year 12, Glen concentrated on his academic work, securing first class honours in Pure Mathematics and second class honours in Physics, Chemistry and Calculus, sufficient to secure him a Commonwealth Scholarship to study at the recently opened Monash University in Clayton.

Glen was at Monash when the campus was small in numbers but was well supplied with personalities and Glen held his own amongst them. His contemporaries included the activist Pete Steedman, writer Julian West (son of novelist

Morris West) and playwright John Romeril. Glen gravitated to the Drama Society and was involved in many productions during his four years at the university.

In those early days at Monash, arts students were required to include a general science subject among their subjects and science students had to include an arts subject amongst theirs. Glen chose history of language as his arts subject and that may well have been what sparked his later interest in languages and counting systems.

In 1965, he graduated with a Bachelor of Science degree and, in the following year, was awarded a Diploma in Education – confirming the prophecy in the school magazine six years earlier.

By 1968, Glen was well settled at the Papua and New Guinea University of Technology where he would spend the next 21 years. His colleagues remember him as a gifted teacher, a true academic, a bibliophile, a gourmet, a dedicated ethnomathematical anthropologist and linguist.

Completely fascinated by variation in counting systems from one ethnic group to another, he began collecting data using a questionnaire completed by students and from talks with village elders. He read old documents written in English, German and Dutch and compared old and new accounts of counting systems and compared systems used by neighbouring groups. He collected the natural language numerals of 883 of the 1200 languages spoken in the region encompassing PNG, West Papua, the Solomon Islands,

Vanuatu, Fiji, New Caledonia, Polynesia and Micronesia.

Glen's study expanded the understanding of counting systems and the history of number and it has illustrated procedures for the analysis of linguistic materials for the study of mathematics.

In 1976, Glen took study leave and travelled extensively to find out all he could about new developments in geometry teaching. A visit to the University of Cambridge led to the completion of a Master of Philosophy degree but he was soon drawn back to PNG. He recognized the urgency of the need to collect and study ethno-mathematical practices in traditional societies because of the rate at which languages and traditional knowledge were dying out.

Glen returned to Australia in 1989 and taught in the Faculty of Education at Deakin University in Geelong. Armed with all of his data, he prepared his PhD thesis "Counting Systems of Papua New Guinea and Oceania" in which he documented over 2000 different counting systems in four massive appendices.

Sadly, ill health caught up with Glen and he died just a week before his 52nd birthday. A special doctoral graduation ceremony was held in Australia, attended by the Vice-Chancellor and Registrar of the PNG University of Technology two weeks before Glen died.

His contributions to learning have been recognized by the creation of the Glen Lean Ethno-mathematics Centre at the University of Goroka and the Glendon A. Lean Memorial

Award at Deakin University, following a bequest from Glen's father.

He may not have been well known in his one year at Caulfield but Glen's contributions to the world of mathematical knowledge and education are recognized throughout the world.

Benjamin Maresh

1976 – 1994

In 1987, Ben followed his older brother, Sam, to Caulfield and involved himself fully in those areas of school life that attracted him – and there were many. He was bright, very bright, and duly won a Headmaster's Commendation for Academic excellence and was involved in the Junior University and the Young Achievers programs.

Helping others featured prominently in Ben's life. He was a leader at the school's farm and outdoor centre at Yarra Junction and took part in the Salvation Army appeals and community service. He received the Tom Rowe Prize for Service and became Vice-Captain of Kurrle House in Year 12.

Ben was not an actor but loved theatre, heading the lighting crews of *My Fair Lady*, *Hello Dolly* and *Joseph and the Amazing Technicolour Dreamcoat*.

He played 2nds volleyball but team sport did not particularly interest him. His Housemaster, Gary Tyler, described him as being more laid back than his older brother but no less aspirational. He enjoyed discussing ethics and to challenge conventional perspectives, like hair length. In the fashion of the time, he parted his hair in the middle and wore it helmet-like and as long as he could get away with. Many will remember his very amusing and accurate impersonations of Jock Nelson, the Chief of Staff.

His teachers remember him as a very creative and musical boy. He loved playing his guitar, art and surfing, his kind of sport. In art, his three-dimensional work was slowly forming and he was fully engaged in making himself better. His art teacher, Ross Brooks, recalls the earnestness of his gaze as Ben quizzed him on how to improve his design work and how, with a dismissive smile, he deflected any praise that came his way.

Ben had the intellectually and aesthetically demanding Max Grierson for art in Year 12. Ross Brooks remembers Max coming into the art staff room talking about how "this kid Ben Maresh" would not only take up the challenges Max laid before him but would pose his own to Max. By the end of Year 12, Max and Ben had developed both an easy rapport and an incredibly productive working relationship.

Ben planned to continue his passion for art at university but decided to defer and travel to Timor, perhaps lured by tales of amazing surfing conditions but also because his father was working at Kupang in West Timor on a project to build a tourist resort.

In mid-April, 1994, the school community was shocked to receive the news that Ben had died in a hotel fire in Kupang. Slowly, very conflicting reports began to emerge.

Ben met up with three other tourists at a party and they ended up staying with him at Nonsui beach, about 12 miles from town. Ten days before he died, Ben took two of his new friends to the airport. On his way back, Ben was hit on the head by one of two people on a motorbike. He followed them into town and was severely beaten by a mob of workers from the Eden Hotel. The manager of the hotel had seen Ben at the airport a number of times and knew his connexion with the resort being built at Nonsui. It is believed that the manager thought that Ben was taking business from him and had him beaten up to "send him a message".

The attack was reported to the police. Ben identified the ringleaders of the mob, including the manager of the hotel but the police refused to arrest anyone.

Fearful for his safety at Nonsui, Ben decided to return to Melbourne. He moved into the Morning Sun Hotel in the heart of Kupang where he thought he would be safe. On the evening of 6th April, Ben was playing his guitar on the hotel verandah until after midnight when he went to his room. Soon afterwards, people at the hotel heard an argument and screaming coming from Ben's room not long before the hotel caught fire. Suspiciously, Ben's door was locked and the hotel's master key was missing. Ben died in his hotel room in the early hours of the morning, not six months after leaving school.

The Kupang police issued a statement that Ben had set fire to himself, smoking in bed while drunk. Robert Maresh brought his son's body back to Australia where an autopsy was conducted. Dr David Ranson, the Assistant Director of Coronial Pathology, reported that Ben was not drunk and the experts on fire deaths at the State Forensic Laboratory suggested that a fire started by a cigarette could not have caused the damage that Ben's body had sustained. After looking at photographs of the fire and the position of Ben's body, Dr Peter Thatcher of the Victorian Forensic Science Centre told the Coroner's Court he could not conclude that the fire started in the bed or in the room where Ben was found.

Coroner Graeme Johnstone found that there was insufficient evidence to make a finding on the cause of Ben's death and, as a result of the lack of evidence, he could not exclude theories to explain Ben's death.

In the ensuing years, Ben's family sought help to find out what really happened to him. Australians in Kupang as well as some locals told them the fire was deliberately lit. The Australians refused to speak to police for fear of losing their Indonesian visas.

The Australian Federal Police stated that they could not investigate criminal matters in foreign jurisdictions, although they had investigated the deaths of Australians in Cambodia. Ben's family sought the support of the Foreign Minister, Senator Gareth Evans, who, a year after Ben's death and some adverse media coverage, finally agreed to meet his family. He told them that his department had done all it could and that there was no hard evidence of foul play.

Ruth Bowes, who owned the hotel in which Ben died, told his family that she believed he had been murdered. It may well be that he was beaten to death and the hotel set alight by the thugs who mistakenly thought that Ben was involved in taking business away from their tourist hotel. We will never know what really happened to Ben but we do know that, at the time and in the years following, Australia did everything it could not to upset the Indonesian government.

With the support of Ben's family, Caulfield created the Benjamin Robert Maresh Prize for Three Dimensional Art. Many recipients of that prize have since gone on to make their mark in the world of art and design – just as Ben would have done.

Pete Pearson

1877 – 1929

In 1928, Edward, Prince of Wales, decided to go on a hunting tour of Uganda and Tanganyika. You may have heard of him. He had a long career as Prince of Wales from 1910 to 1936 then a very short career as King Edward VIII in 1936 and thereafter a very long career as a royal outcast until his death in 1972.

Sport was the Prince's main recreation. He hunted foxes in England, went pig-sticking in India and shot big game in

Africa. To hunt in Uganda, the Prince sought the services of the best hunting guide in East Africa. His name was Pete Pearson.

Pete was born in Melbourne and was enrolled at Caulfield in 1889 but, by the age of 18, he had left school, left Melbourne and had gone in search of adventure.

Not frightened of a hard or dirty job, he worked, at various times, as a shearer and as a miner before joining a ship's company bound for South Africa and the Boer War. He literally jumped ship off Durban, swam to shore and joined a cavalry unit.

Seeing no reason to return to Australia, he decided that elephant hunting sounded like it could be fun and profitable. Initially, he hunted in Uganda but new game quotas limited hunters to three elephants a year so Pete adopted a different approach – hunting illegally in another area where the Belgian authorities exercised little control. He hunted there until 1910 when the territory returned to British control and quotas were enforced.

Word was out that life for hunters was easier in the Congo where the French and Belgian authorities still issued licences for up to 30 elephants a year.

Germany had a long-standing colony in East Africa and the British government was concerned that the German colonial authorities would arm local tribes and cause unrest between them. With extensive knowledge of the East African bush and experience in dealing with local tribesmen, Pete was commissioned as a Lieutenant in the East Africa Protectorate's Intelligence Department with which he served until the end of the war in 1918.

With the war behind him, Pete returned to hunting, at first in Tanganyika but, when quotas were reduced, he went to Uganda where the government had set up a Game Department in an effort to combat destruction to fences and crops caused by elephants and thereby preventing the development of agriculture. Pete was assigned to the West Nile province, an area he knew very well. A salary of £50 was provided and the Governor, Sir William Gowers, appointed Pete and the game wardens in charge of the other provinces as Colonial Civil Servants, assuring a lifetime pension. This was good news for Pete who had never been particularly good at looking after money.

In 1924, Pete accompanied the safari for the Duke and Duchess of York (later King George VI and Queen Elizabeth) as a hunting guide during their visit to Uganda. The Duke and Duchess must have been happy with Pete's guiding because he was charged with organizing an eight-day hunting safari for the Prince of Wales in 1928.

On the last day of the safari, the royal party was on the trail of a bull elephant when they were suddenly charged by another bull. Pete pushed the Prince out of harm's way and then he and another guide both fired at the charging elephant which fell dead not six yards from the Prince. Sir William Gowers later wrote, "It was an exhibition of presence of mind, quickness and courage which I am glad to have been privileged to witness, and which none of those who saw it will ever forget". As symbols of his gratitude, the Prince presented Pete with a tie pin bearing the Prince's cypher and a pair of cufflinks.

In 1929, Pete became ill and was diagnosed with stomach cancer. He died on 10th September. Pete's friends contributed to a fund for a memorial which was located on a rise overlooking Lake Albert. It depicts two elephants on a hill, facing each other with a palm tree between them. Below is the simple inscription PETE PEARSON MCMXXIX. It is not surprising that the Prince of Wales was one of the first contributors to the fund.

Robert Grieve, VC

1889 – 1957

Robert Cuthbert Grieve, the first old-boy of a Victorian Public School to win a Victoria Cross, came to Caulfield in 1899 at the age of ten. Aside from the fact that he was born on 19th June 1889, the son of Anne and John Grieve and lived at *Erne Lodge* in Bay Street, North Brighton, we know very little about Bob's early life except that he and his younger brother, John, went on to Wesley College but Bob was only there for two years. He played football and cricket at school and was a member of the Brighton District Cricket Association in its founding season of 1907-08 when he was the club's highest wicket taker.

After Bob left school, he became an interstate commercial traveller in the softgoods field but found time for military service as a citizen-soldier in the Victorian Rangers. On 17th January 1916, he was commissioned as a Second-Lieutenant in the newly raised 37th Battalion. Shortly after, he was promoted to Lieutenant and embarked for overseas with the battalion on 1st June. The Great War had been raging in Europe for nearly two years and the first anniversary of the landing at Gallipoli had already passed by. The 37th Battalion was part of the 3rd Division which trained on Salisbury Plain in England before moving to France in November 1916.

Bob displayed considerable qualities of leadership and, in February 1917, was appointed an acting Captain, the rank being confirmed on 9th April when he was given command of "A" Company, just in time to lead it into battle at Messines in June.

It was at the battle of Messines that the Australian soldiers encountered "blockhouse" fighting for the first time. These "blockhouses" were built of reinforced concrete with firing slits for machine-gun crews and were scattered all over the Messines front. Because of their odd shape, the soldiers called them "pill-boxes".

From one of these "pill-boxes" came the fire which struck Bob's company just as it was moving through a gap in the wire in front of the German trench under attack on 7th June. Very soon after, half of the men and all of the officers except Bob had been struck down. As the official citation for his Victoria Cross tells us:

Captain Grieve gave orders for the company to push on, and dashed off himself towards the spot from which the machine gun fire was coming. He had to cover about 50 yards of open ground under the direct observation of the enemy, who fired at him continuously, but without success. He reached the doorway from which one of the guns was firing, and threw bomb after bomb inside, until both machine guns were silenced. With his revolver he killed the remainder of the crews. He then searched both the house and its neighbourhood thoroughly, to ensure that none of the enemy had escaped him, and afterwards re-joined his company. With characteristic coolness and ability he reorganized his men, and entered the German trenches at their head. It was entirely due to him that the assault was carried to a successful conclusion. By his utter disregard of danger, his coolness under fire, and his magnificent conduct throughout the whole of the operations, he set a splendid example to the non-commissioned officers and men of his company, and when he finally fell wounded, the position was in our hands, and the few men that remained of the enemy were in flight.

The Victoria Cross is usually awarded on the recommendation of senior officers but, in Bob's case, all the other officers were killed. As a result, a most unusual thing occurred. The men of his company sent a letter to the authorities, making the recommendation. This unconventional nomination was accepted and the award duly made.

The shoulder wound he received at Messines kept him in hospital in England for six months. Whilst he was recuperating, he received the following letter, signed by every member of "A" Company of the 37th Battalion:

> *Sir,*
>
> *NCOs and men of your Company, and especially those who had the honour of being led into action at the Battle of Messines, wish to take this the earliest opportunity to congratulate you upon the very high and distinguished honour it has pleased His Majesty the King to confer upon you at this time, and also the honour of bringing to our battalion the first VC. We, as men of your Company will cherish with pride your deeds of heroism and devotion which stimulate us to go forward in the face of all danger and at critical moments to give the right guidance that won the day and added to the banner of Australia, a name which time will never obliterate. We trust that your recovery may be a speedy one, and we can assure you that there awaits you, on your return to the boys, a very hearty welcome.*

Such was the admiration his men had for him. A quiet, self-effacing man, Bob described the incident with characteristic understatement:

> *The company was held up by fire from machine-guns in a concrete building. These were put out of action by the aid of Mills grenades and the company was able to go forward on to the objective allotted to us.*

When he was discharged from hospital, Bob re-joined his unit which, by then, had been relocated in France. Bob was plagued with illness and was diagnosed with serious inflammation of the kidneys. He was admitted to the 2nd Australian Casualty Clearing Station where he was looked after by a member of the Australian Army Nursing Service, Sister May Isobel Bowman.

Sister Bowman and Captain Grieve were married in Sydney on 7th August, 1918. Bob had been repatriated to Australia as medically unfit for further service.

The Grieves settled in Melbourne where Bob went back into the softgoods business, founding the firm of Grieve, Gardner and Company.

When war broke out in 1939, Bob again volunteered his services. He was appointed a Captain in the 4th Victorian Battalion of the Volunteer Defence Corps in June, 1942, with which he served until he was placed on the Retired List on 18th September, 1944.

Bob collapsed at work and died of heart failure on 4th October 1957. His Victoria Cross was presented to the Shrine of Remembrance in Melbourne in 2003 where it is the centrepiece in a display of some 7,000 medals. It is one of the few Victoria Crosses on display that is not at the Australian War Memorial in Canberra.

Sir John Behan

1881 – 1957

John Clifford Valentine Behan was born on 8th May 1881, the year in which Caulfield Grammar School was founded. He was the ninth child of William and Phoebe Behan of Footscray, When John was ten years of age, his parents were living in one of the terrace houses on the corner of Regent Street and Glen Eira Road in East St Kilda. He watched the comings and goings of the pupils of the school and, on many occasions, climbed with one of his sisters the gum trees in the large paddock, part of which now forms the site of the present Caulfield Campus buildings. On early autumn mornings, the Behan children would search the paddock for mushrooms, as would many other children of the district.

Shortly afterwards, the Behan family moved to a house in Balaclava Road near the St Kilda Town Hall, and later to Gordon Street in Elsternwick. It was whilst living in Gordon Street that John contracted typhoid fever and was lucky to recover.

From an early age, John had wanted to go to Caulfield but he knew that, because his family was quite poor, the only way he would be able to do so was by winning a scholarship. Unfortunately, the depression of the early 1890s meant the suspension of State School Scholarships. Heads of secondary schools were not pleased with this eventuality so they clubbed together to offer places in their schools, provided that the winners were accorded the status of State School Scholars. John sat the examination but, sadly, his name did not appear in the published list of winners. Despite this, Mrs Behan received an offer of a half scholarship from the Headmaster, the Reverend E.J. Barnett, which set the family the task of raising half the school fees (then just under £30).

John enrolled in February, 1894, and was placed in Form 4A. He set out with a fixed determination to show that Mr Barnett's faith in him was not misplaced. On Speech Day in 1895, John was announced as Dux, having caught up with all of the full scholars of 1894 and passing Matriculation along with them. He returned the following year to do honours work in English and history. He was taught English by J.F. McKeddie who spent some years as a schoolmaster to earn enough money to enable him to study medicine. Eventually McKeddie became a senior Collins Street specialist. History was under the charge of James Sutherland, a member of a distinguished academic family of the time. His brother, Alexander, became Registrar of the University of Melbourne in 1902. His final year at Caulfield earned John a university exhibition, valued at £80 a year and tenable for four years.

In 1897, he entered Trinity College of the University of Melbourne with a resident exhibition which he held for two years. He went on to win the Clarke Resident Scholarship and three non-foundation resident scholarships.

Between 1897 and 1904, John gained almost every academic honour available to him. He won the Wyselaskie Scholarships in English Constitutional History and Political Economy, the Hastie Exhibition in Deductive Logic, the Hastie Scholarship in Logic and Philosophy and the Cobden Club Medal in Political Economy. He graduated Bachelor of Arts with first-class honours in logic and philosophy and in political economy. He also gained a Bachelor of Laws degree with first-class honours, winning the Supreme Court Prize. During 1904, John worked as a resident tutor at Trinity College. In the same year, he was named as Victoria's first Rhodes Scholar.

A Rhodes Scholarship is a rare honour. Only one is allocated to each state in the Commonwealth each year. In selecting Scholars, the selection committee must have regard to academic ability, character and involvement in games. The chosen Scholar is rewarded with the chance to spend several years studying at Oxford University.

John's academic career at Oxford was equally as brilliant as it had been at Melbourne. Reading law at Hertford College, he took first-class honours in his Bachelor of Arts degree in jurisprudence and in his Bachelor of Civil Laws degree. He won both the Vinerian and Eldon Law Scholarships and secured first-class honours in his Bar final examinations in the Middle Temple. His Oxford prizes were valued at over £6,000, a huge sum of money in those days.

John returned home in 1907 for a short visit during which he married Violet Greta Caldwell of Brighton. They returned to Oxford shortly afterwards so that John could take up his appointment as lecturer in law in University College where, in 1909, he was awarded the Stowell Civil Law Fellowship. *The Caulfield Grammarian* of 1911 was convinced that there was little hope that John would ever return to live in Australia. One of the magazine's reporters had found an article in the *British Australasian* of 27th July announcing that "Mr Behan, LL.B., the first Victorian Rhodes Scholar, is building a house in Oxford". His return seemed even less likely when, in 1914, he was appointed Dean of University College, a lay officer responsible for the discipline of the college.

The Great War broke out in the first week of August 1914 and John's services were taken up by the ministries of munitions, food and national service with which he shared his time with Oxford University until 1917. In that year, it became clear that Dr Alexander Leeper, Warden of Trinity College in the University of Melbourne, planned to retire. John applied for the position and was very strongly supported by leading educationists in Australia and England. His application was successful and he took up the wardenship in March 1918 at 36 years of age.

The Behans returned to Australia by a circuitous route. The only ship available was a 50-year-old Allan liner which they boarded in the Mersey. The journey was undertaken with some trepidation as the German submarine campaign was at its peak. They were to cross the Atlantic to the United States and then make their way to Melbourne. Shortly after boarding the liner, they found themselves in the company of John's former headmaster, the Reverend E.J. Barnett. Mr and Mrs Barnett were on their way back to the Far East. After leaving Caulfield, Barnett had become the founding headmaster of St Stephen's College in Hong Kong. Together, the Barnetts and Behans passed a pleasant and uneventful voyage.

On arrival at Trinity, Behan found the buildings in disrepair and the college seriously short of funds. He set about to solve both of these problems. By the end of 1919, he had raised £120,000 and a further £50,000 by 1925. Moves by influential friends of the college to limit the control exercised by the Anglican clergy increased John's difficulties in convincing the council that Trinity should become an incorporated body, governed on the Oxford model by a provost and fellows, instead of by an external council.

John also had other problems on his hands. There had always been a tradition of hostility towards the Warden at Trinity and this was exacerbated in 1930 when the students' club opposed all disciplinary measures. Despite a widespread prohibitionist sentiment in the community, John resisted closing the college's buttery until incidents in 1933 forced him to do so. The club then adopted a policy "directed to procuring the removal of the Warden". The council supported John but decided to postpone any consideration of incorporation whilst John was Warden.

The appointment of a Dean in 1933 helped remove John from day-to-day contact with the students and this allowed him to do the things he did well. He introduced his students to the richness of the English language, to good music and set before them an example of good manners, self-discipline and singleness of purpose. He soon earned their respect and affection.

His own academic development had not been forgotten. In 1924, he published in London *The use of land as affected by covenants* which earned him the degree of Doctor of Laws from the University of Melbourne.

From 1921 to 1952, John served as secretary to the Rhodes Trust in Australia and greatly streamlined the working of its selection committees. He also served on the council of Caulfield Grammar School from 1931 to 1938.

During the Second World War, John relieved the wartime

financial problems of the college by arranging for its part-occupation by the Royal Australian Air Force. When the war was over, he conducted another highly successful fund-raising campaign for renovations. In early 1946, he attempted, once again, to obtain self-government but again he failed. He felt that he had no option but to resign and did so in June of that year. His record at Trinity was impressive: he had raised over £280,000 in endowments and secured the future of the university college as an important element in university development. There can be no doubt that John had made Trinity the nearest in Australia to the ideal of an Oxford or Cambridge college.

John spent his retirement at Olinda, in the hills just out of Melbourne. King George VI honoured him with a knighthood in 1949. Sir John Behan died at Olinda on 30th September 1957. Once asked to nominate the most important thing he had learnt, he said, "In the battle of life mere brains do not count as much as the ability to make friends, to pick the right ones and, above all, to keep them".

Helen Vimpani

1925 – 2014

Helen Vimpani joined the small office staff at Caulfield in 1959. It was a busy place and the office staff looked after what was called the Big School at Glen Eira Road, the junior school, Shaw House which was in Mayfield Street, a five-minute stroll away, and Yarra Junction. A small army carries out these roles today.

Early in that same year, Mrs Kemp, the headmaster's secretary, advised her boss of her intention to retire. Perhaps trying to deny the inevitability of Mrs Kemp's departure, Stan Kurrle, uncharacteristically, moved at a snail's pace to find a successor. Helen, already working in the office, applied for the job and was successful.

Helen was educated at Korowa where her school reports regularly rated her as an above average student but she always insisted that she was no scholar. Leaving school at 16, she first turned her hand at training to be a mothercraft nurse at St Gabriel's in Kew but found it hard to live in so she left and took up a position with the Bank of Australasia in St Kilda Road. Other jobs followed, at the Eye and Ear Hospital and with Elder Smith and Co.

Her regular games of golf were suspended in 1956 when she was diagnosed with tuberculosis and required major surgery and a long convalescence. As her health improved, she found a job which was not too onerous and fitted with her love of children; she became governess to two boys and a girl on a farm at Deniliquin.

In his Speech Night report at the end of 1959, Stan Kurrle praised both Mrs Kemp and Helen. He told his audience, "Mrs Kemp left her work in such a methodical way that Miss Vimpani picked up the threads with scarcely a break in routine". And so it would run for another 26 years.

As well as taking over the role of headmaster's secretary,

Helen was in charge of enrolments for Shaw House and the Big School as well as Malvern when it came under Caulfield's management in 1961. When it was announced that Caulfield would open a co-educational campus at Wheelers Hill in 1981, enrolments became a full-time job and a registrar was appointed. Helen understood the need to give up this part of her work but missed the early contact with prospective parents and their children.

Although she could have become isolated from contact with the students in her re-shaped role as secretary to the headmaster, the reality was quite the reverse. Helen took an interest in all student activities: walkathons, fund-raising, the Theatre Guild, music, lunchtime stalls, social services and the Cadet Unit. All captured her interest and she helped out in myriad ways. In 1980, she joined staff and students on an 18-day tour of Indonesia.

Helen was patient, well organized, disliked rush and haste, enjoyed the "people" side of her job and was liked by both teachers and boys. She was able to calm the most irate of masters who may have wanted the headmaster to punish a particular boy. She achieved this by keeping him sitting on an uncomfortable chair in a noisy office until his anger had subsided – and only then finding the headmaster.

Stan Kurrle left Caulfield at the end of 1964 and Bruce Lumsden took up the reins. He soon realised his good fortune in having Helen as his secretary. In his report to Council at the end of his first year he said, "Some years of experience had already taught me that, next to a good wife, an administrator needs most an efficient secretary. In Miss Helen Vimpani, I have found a secretary who in versatility, temperament and competence is second to none".

The late 60s and 70s were not an easy time for schools. This was the era of the alternative society, hippies, long hair, rebellion, Nick Cave (yes, he went to Caulfield) and every breakaway movement you can imagine. Helen managed to take it all in her stride.

Angas Holmes had been headmaster for four years when Wheelers Hill Campus opened in 1981, the school's centenary year. Keeping tabs on the headmaster's whereabouts became an even greater problem. He could have been at Glen Eira Road, Malvern, Wheelers Hill, Yarra Junction or in transit.

When leave accrued, Helen made good use of it. In 1976, she travelled to England and Europe, particularly enjoying a sojourn in the Greek Islands. In 1983, she took a second trip to England and Europe.

In 1985, Helen celebrated a quarter of a century of service to Caulfield and she announced that she would retire at the end of the year. It was not only then that honours came her way. In 1976, the school's boat club had named a boat the *Helen Vimpani*. Honorary Life Membership of the Parents and Friends' Association was awarded and she was also made an Honorary Life Member of the Caulfield Grammarians' Association, the first female to receive such an honour in the school's then 104 year history.

Helen's connexion with Caulfield did not end there. She had

made lifelong friends and maintained regular contact with them, no matter in what part of the world they lived.

That three headmasters should have equally valued her services is remarkable. Each of them had appreciated her loyalty, unflappability, concern for her boss, and her uncomplicated niceness.

Finlay Crisp

1917 – 1984

Leslie Finlay Crisp was born at Sandringham on 19th January, 1917. He started school at Black Rock State School, the school nearest his parents' home in Sandringham, and progressed to Caulfield in February 1929. His father was obliged to go to Adelaide for work and the family followed, with the exception of Fin who stayed until the end of the year with his aunt and grandmother. In the one year he spent at Caulfield, Fin made quite an impression. The headmaster, Frank Archer, provided Fin's father with a reference on 16th January 1930, describing Fin as "a fine type of boy, having excellent ability and being a hard worker. He was Dux of his form and took a keen interest in all school activities. His character is exemplary".

Fin arrived at St Peter's College, Adelaide, at the start of 1930 and set about the business of involving himself in a wide range of school activities although, apart from swimming, he was not prominent in sport.

1935 saw Fin's arrival at St Mark's College in the University of Adelaide. In September of that year, he was awarded the League of Nations Prize for his essay entitled *Russia and the League*.

During his four years at Adelaide, Fin achieved excellent academic results. He won the Economics Society Prize and the Harold Fisher Bursary. He was a member of the University Union Committee and co-founder in 1937 of the National Union of Australian University Students. He led the university's debating team to victory at the Intervarsity tournament in Melbourne in 1938. He became co-editor of *On Dit*, the student newspaper, in 1937 and co-editor of *Phoenix*, a student literary magazine in 1938. On the basis of his final results, he was awarded a Tinline Scholarship for Postgraduate Research.

During his third year at Adelaide, on 12th October 1937, Fin lodged the necessary application form for the award of Rhodes Scholarships, offering himself as a candidate for 1938. In his personal statement, attached to the official application form, Fin indicated that his interests had lain increasingly in the study of politics for the previous five years and that it was his ambition eventually to enter political life. He believed that a Rhodes Scholarship would give him the opportunity to carry his work further. He advised the Scholarship Selection Committee that he would read for Honours Schools in philosophy, politics and economics (Modern Greats) and that "the opportunity of coming into direct contact with political and social life in England and, if possible, on the Continent, and of profiting by Oxford life in general would [be] valuable to me. Equally invaluable would be the chance of knowing men of similar interests drawn to Oxford from countries which I may never be able to visit".

Among his referees were Professor G.V. Portus and Professor J.A. La Nauze who had both been Rhodes Scholars and gave Fin glowing references. Another referee was A.S. Blackburn, an Adelaide solicitor who had won the Victoria Cross at Pozières in 1916 and who was to become a distinguished military leader in the 1939-45 War. Blackburn stated that Fin's "qualities of manhood are of an extremely high standard and all through his school career as well as at the university, he has shown that he possesses the quality of leadership – a quality I may add, which he has always exercised in the direction of high ideals of living and honour".

One imagines that the committee did not have too much trouble in deciding to award the 1937 South Australian Rhodes Scholarship to Leslie Finlay Crisp. The only weakness in his application lay in the sporting area as he was not a "star" player. Professor Portus deflected that criticism in his reference when he said, "I do not think [that] matters very greatly so long as a man plays games".

Fin was off to Balliol College, Oxford, where he remained until 1940. By then, the Second World War was well under way. He chose not to take out a wartime (shortened) degree and returned to Australia.

Fin entered the Public Service and was employed in Melbourne until 1941 in the Australian Shortwave Broadcasting Service. In the same year, the University of Adelaide awarded him the John L. Young Research Scholarship and approved the subject of his thesis for the degree of Master of Arts. The thesis was entitled "The Parliamentary Government of the Commonwealth with special reference to the effect of Australian conditions upon traditional British Parliamentary institutions and practices". The degree was conferred *in absentia* in 1948. The thesis was the basis of his book *Parliamentary Government of the Commonwealth of Australia* which appeared in 1949 and, in one form or another, remained in print for the next 40 years.

In late 1941, Fin transferred to the Department of Labour and National Service's Reconstruction Research Division and in 1942 he moved to the Department of Post-War Reconstruction. Ben Chifley was appointed Minister for Post-War Reconstruction in December 1942 and chose H.C. Coombs to be his Director-General. The war had not yet reached its peak in terms of Australia's war effort but a start on post-war reconstruction had to be made. It had to be quiet, exploratory, methodical and unspectacular. Chifley had the temperament which matched the demands of the situation and saw that appropriate men were appointed to carry out the necessary tasks.

From 1943 to 1945, Fin was (with Paul Hasluck) Joint Secretary of the Inter-Departmental Committee on External Relations and in 1945 he became a member of Frank Forde's group in the delegation to San Francisco for the founding conference of the United Nations. In 1944 and 1945, Fin began teaching again as a part-time lecturer to diplomatic cadets at Canberra University College. In 1947, he became Acting Secretary of the Interim Council of the Australian National University.

After the war and seven years as a civil servant, Fin returned to Oxford for the 1947-48 academic year. He took out his degree with first-class honours, had been Treasurer of the Union and President of the Ralegh Club and had certainly fulfilled the promise that his scholarship referees had seen in him a decade earlier.

On his return to Australia from Oxford, Fin resumed his work with the Department of Post-War Reconstruction and, in 1949, became Director-General. By this time, the Australian Labour Party was on its way out of office and along with it went much of Fin's plan for a career in politics.

In 1950, Fin took up the foundation Chair and Departmental Headship in Political Science at Canberra University College. The appointment had been made in May 1949 but he had deferred taking up the post at the express wish of the Prime Minister. Professor Crisp, as he now was, later took the same Chair in the School of General Studies when Canberra University College merged with the Australian National University.

The relationship between the College and the University must have been an unusual one. In his autobiography, Russel Ward writes that in 1953 "The Australian National

University might well have been the smallest institution of its kind in the world. There were only seven departments concerned with the humanities: History, Pacific History, Law, Politics, Social Philosophy, Anthropology, and International Relations. And, best of all, each department was then supported by only one or two (rarely three) teachers and, as likely as not, even fewer post-graduate students. Scholars anywhere can rarely have had it so good . . . Organizationally 'the College' was a small branch of the University of Melbourne, but not so small that it did not have more academic staff and many more students, albeit undergraduates, than the ANU. With Manning Clark in the Chair of History and A.D. Hope in that of English, many thought the College staff more distinguished, if less puffed-up, than that of the post-graduate research institution".

In 1955, Fin published *The Australian Federal Labour Party*. The book had been completed early in 1953, well before the 1954-57 split in the party which led to the founding of the Democratic Labour Party which kept the ALP out of office until December 1972. The book is a history of the internal constitutional and organizational development of the party from 1901 to 1951 and is not and never was intended to be a general history of the party during that period.

Fin's book on the Labour Party was followed in 1960 by his biography of Ben Chifley and in 1966 by *Australian National Government* which is still considered a standard work. He spent from 1960 to 1970 building and managing a large department in the Australian National University. By

1970, the hard work was taking its toll on his health and he decided to step down as Head of Department.

Ian Wilson of ANU wrote that Fin "was often characterised as conservative and did not shrink from the rightist label within the ALP, but his was an older Labour view in which equality of opportunity and access in education were vitally important. He took great pains to overcome what he saw as the deprivations students from rural or industrial suburban backgrounds brought with them to university . . . groups of undergraduates would be brought home to meet his family and be introduced to his other great love, that of good books. These acts were paternal rather than paternalistic and were never patronising. He remained active within the local ALP and his criticisms of it again had their roots in his impressions of the 1930s. He deplored the white-collar colonialism of the party and was just as outspoken in his attacks on student radicalism when its social base was the middle class".

As Ian Wilson mentioned, Fin had a passion for books and built up an enormous collection. In 1982, Helen Crisp reflected on his library thus:

> He has a very spacious study in the garden at the back
> That's crammed up to the ceiling with his treasured books; in fact
> They've spread too, to the living room, the bedrooms and the hall
> While mine are in the kitchen where I'm driven up the wall.

Historian Manning Clark had first met Fin at Belgrave in the late 1920s and again at Oxford in 1928. Working with him in Canberra he felt that Fin "had never been able to make up his mind whether to be a scholar, a public servant or a Labour Leader . . . Many things delighted him – a victory for Collingwood in a football game, a victory for Australia in a test cricket game, a Labour victory . . . He was at his happiest washing up with a bunch of students or members of his local Labour Party branch, or taking the tea-towel from his hostess at the end of a dinner party. There he bubbled over with warmth and affection for those he liked". One cannot, however, always trust what historians tell us. Helen Crisp pointed out to me that Fin, inexplicably, always barracked for England when playing a cricket test against Australia!

On 20th February 1974, the Federal Treasurer, Frank Crean, announced that the Governor-General in Council had appointed Professor L.F. Crisp a member of the Board of the Commonwealth Banking Corporation. A year later, on 14th February 1975, the new Treasurer, Dr Jim Cairns, announced Fin's appointment as chairman of the bank's board, an office he held until his death on 21st December 1984. Fin had retired from the Chair of Political Science in 1977 but retained his links with the university in a number of ways. In 1978, he was appointed an Honorary Research Fellow in the Department of Political Science and he remained a member of the Board of Directors of the University Co-operative Bookshop until 1979. He had been a member of that board since 1973 and was always keen to make books more widely available.

After he had retired from teaching, he worked on a study of political leaders and political leadership in Australia.

Between 1979 and 1984, he produced six monographs on the Federation period. These were published by Melbourne University Press in 1990 under the title *Federation Fathers*.

By any measurement, Fin was an outstanding Australian. A worker for all of his 67 years as student, civil servant, teacher and administrator, Fin suffered a heart attack and died after a strenuous day and a publishing occasion after work. He died "in harness" and, one suspects, he would have wanted it that way. Manning Clark's words from his foreword to *Federation Fathers* provide a fitting tribute: "Fin devoted his great talents and energies to educating Australians about their political institutions . . . His published work stands as a monument to his faith. The thousands of students he influenced play their part in handing on the message he presented to them with such eloquence".

He is commemorated in the City of Canberra by the Finlay Crisp Centre and by the L.F. Crisp building on the ANU campus.

Don Wirth

1928 – 2014

Don was born in Melbourne on 30th September 1928. He attended Prahran Technical School from 1941 to 1943 and moved to Caulfield in Year 10. He played First XI cricket for two years and, in 1946, was Form Captain of Year 12 and a leader of the Christian group Crusader Union.

He began teacher training in 1947 and lived in Caulfield's boarding house as a resident master. He stayed on at Caulfield to teach and began coaching cricket in 1951, taking the First XI to four Associated Grammar School cricket premierships.

There can be little doubt that Don's greatest contribution to Caulfield came in the 1960s when headmaster Bruce Lumsden appointed him Master of the Middle School. He set about reforming the teaching of mathematics and science, placing them in a real-world context. His Middle School program of experiential learning, excursions and their reporting soon came to the attention of educators in other parts of Australia and overseas.

The success of Don's work was demonstrated by reference to his programs in Dr Henry Schoenheimer's book *Good Australian Schools and their Communities* and in a 30-minute video of students in the mathematics room and the related excursions, made by the Faculty of Education at Monash University. Don was invited to speak at the International Conference of Mathematics Teachers in Germany, wrote two textbooks, became a councillor with the Schools Commission Innovations Program and sat on the national committee in Canberra.

Throughout Don's working life, a camera was always at hand and many aspects of school life were recorded by him. He was an excellent photographer and, in 1957, he captured the first photograph in the world of the Russian satellite Sputnik, which was published on the front page of *The Age*.

After 34 years at Caulfield as student and teacher, Don

became Headmaster of the Junior School at Scotch College in 1977. As soon as he arrived, he set about encouraging staff and boys to develop links with the world outside the classroom. The necessary financial and logistical support was provided, grade-level co-ordinators were appointed and classrooms were redesigned. Before long, parents became involved in the classroom, on excursions and on camps.

Don encouraged staff and boys to develop programs and extension of gifted students took place. He developed a computer annexe in 1985 to capitalise on the growth of computer education. Don understood the value of sport and recreation and he strove to have all boys take part in one activity or another, often photographing their endeavours.

At the end of 1985, Don left Scotch to take up the post of Director of Junior Secondary at The King David School where he set up the Middle School. At the beginning of 1989, he moved to Melbourne Girls' Grammar School where he taught mathematics and photography, a post he held until 1997.

Don joined the board of Rossbourne School in Hawthorn, a school for disabled children, in 1986 and was elected president in 1989. When he retired from the board, the school had expanded significantly in numbers and in area.

In 1997, Don reconnected with Caulfield and spent the next 15 years as a volunteer, assisting with the school's pictorial archives and reunion program, undertakings he enjoyed immensely. In recognition of his work, he was inducted as a Fellow of the Caulfield Grammarians' Association in 2003.

Don died on 11th July 2014. To commemorate his lifelong contributions to the school, the Caulfield Grammarians' Association struck the Don Wirth Medal which is presented annually to those who have given distinguished service to the Association.

Bill O'Halloran

1934 – 1994

Looking back at Bill's obituary which I wrote for the English magazine *The Cricketer* in 1995, I noticed that it was rather full of statistics. On reflection, it was probably a very good way to tell at least part of his story.

Born in Corowa, New South Wales, Bill O'Halloran arrived at Caulfield in 1950 at the age of 16. He very quickly established himself as one of those extraordinary boys who could do almost anything and do it very well.

Bill was a good student but it was his sporting ability which drew a lot of attention. He began school in 1950 after term had started, in time to play in only two First XI games. In the match against Ivanhoe Grammar School he took 4/15 and 7/0, statistics which made everyone sit up and take notice. He also played First XVIII football in his first year, including a snap goal in the last moments of the match against Brighton Grammar to win the game.

In the following year, Bill made 255 runs for the First XI and took 29 wickets. He was appointed a School Officer, rather like an apprentice Prefect, and received School Colours for both cricket and football.

In 1952, he was appointed Captain of Cricket, giving excellent performances with the bat and ball. The Sporting Section of *The Argus* of Monday 10th March, reported "Caulfield Grammar School cricket captain, Bill O'Halloran, bowled brilliantly to take ten wickets in the Associated Grammar Schools match against Trinity Grammar School on Saturday". He again played First XVIII football, was a member of the inter-school athletics team and was appointed a Prefect at the start of the year.

To say that he was a hero in his final year at school is something of an understatement. As Captain of Cricket for the second year, there was much celebration when he took his 50th wicket for the school. (He took one more before the season ended.) He was, of course a Prefect again and also Captain of Football and Captain of Buntine House.

Going to the University of Melbourne in 1954 must have seemed, at first, like a rest break. He graduated with a Bachelor of Commerce degree in 1958 and then returned to Caulfield to teach for two years, with many students well aware of him as the sporting hero of just a few years earlier.

Over the next four years, Bill completed teacher training at Mercer House and qualified as an Associate of the Australian Society of Accountants, all the while playing cricket for the St Kilda Cricket Club which he had joined in his final year at Caulfield. He was, in fact, one of the most prolific run-scorers in Melbourne grade cricket in the 21 years he played for St Kilda, captaining the premiership side in 1964-65, making a total of 5,368 runs and taking 312 wickets as a consistent and accurate fast bowler. He was seven times Club Champion.

In 1963, he had returned to Caulfield after a stint in the commercial world, teaching senior commerce subjects, coaching cricket and football and leading Buntine House. He was appointed Housemaster of Buntine in 1966.

When I was in Year 12 in 1964, I remember Bill giving me a thorough bollocking for not turning out for house football practice. I explained to him that it would have been rather difficult as I had turned out for house rugby practice which was on at exactly the same time. I don't think he considered rugby to be much of an excuse.

Bill was rather busy at the start of the year as he had been selected to play cricket for Victoria in the 1962-63 season in which he played six matches. He made a total of 115 runs at an average of 12.77 with a top score of 31. He took four wickets for 202 runs at an average of 50.5 and held four catches. This did no harm to his status with the boys at Caulfield – or the staff, quite a few of whom had taught him.

In 1985, Cricket Victoria created its 200 Club to recognize players who had participated in a combined total of at least 200 VCA First XI, Victorian first-class and test matches. Bill was duly inducted having played 256 eligible matches.

By the end of 1966, Bill had decided to move on from teaching.

He became a well-regarded educational psychologist and also established a niche market consultancy, placing overseas students in Australian schools. This latter aspect of his work grew and grew and through it he made a substantial contribution to the reputation of Australia as a centre of educational excellence. From 1974 to 1992, he was Student Counsellor at the Peninsula School, Mount Eliza.

Peter Coldham

1919 – 1995

His father's chance appointment as manager of a gold mine at Wood's Point led Peter Coldham on the path to Caulfield Grammar School. Peter was born in Sydney in 1919, the son of a mining engineer. He came to Victoria in 1924 and, after his work at Wood's Point had concluded, he settled in Melbourne and enrolled Peter at St Kilda Park State School where he was a contemporary of Zelman Cowen. From St Kilda Park, he went to Caulfield Central School and then to Caulfield Grammar School, starting in class 4B, memorable for being Lester Seward's first class at the school.

In that first year, Peter was Dux of 4B, a feat which he remembered as a highlight of what he described to me, rather modestly, as "an otherwise undistinguished academic career".

By the time he came to Caulfield, Peter had an already developed interest in the law. His great-uncle, Walter

Coldham, who had been educated at Hamilton College and Melbourne Grammar School, was a leading Melbourne barrister in the latter part of the previous century. Walter's brother, Russell, was a barrister in Ballarat. This interest was fuelled by Peter's habit of visiting the courts in his spare time to listen to the great jury advocates of the day.

In 1935, Peter became a School Prefect and Captain of Davies House. In the same year, he captained the First XI, and the school magazine of that year commends him as an effective slow bowler and an excellent batsman. He had played in the First XI since 1933 when he was 14 and made his first century (116) against Carey in 1935.

The following year, Peter was appointed Captain of the School and continued as Captain of Davies House. He showed great form in the First XI and in the third match of the season made another century when he scored 106 not out against Carey. Although he had not played senior football before, he trained with the First XVIII squad and was soon included in the team. In the last match of the season, against Malvern, he played on the wing and his performance was described by the School Magazine's reporter as "one of the finest we have seen".

He particularly enjoyed his role as Captain of the School which required him to represent the school in all sorts of ways. There were receptions at Government House and a wide variety of other social engagements as well as the high ceremony of the combined Anglican schools' services at St Paul's Cathedral.

In 1937, Peter began reading law at the University of Melbourne. He enjoyed his years at university very much and it was there that he developed many friendships which lasted throughout his life. In the middle of his third year, war had begun in Europe and in 1940 Peter joined the RAAF Reserve which required some night study which was conducted, of all places, at Caulfield Grammar School. In 1941, he had commenced Articles but, after three months, was called up in the RAAF on a full-time basis.

His first posting was to Somers for initial training and then to the Royal Showgrounds from May until August when he embarked on a circuitous trip to Rhodesia for flying training. He left with 114 others in the *Queen Elizabeth* and travelled to Suez then in the *Mauretania* to Durban where they had a fortnight's break. The next leg was by train to Bulawayo where flying training took place from October 1941 until the end of 1942. The pilots trained initially in Tiger Moths and then moved to Oxfords for intermediate and advanced training and then "graduated" with 40 hours on Harvards.

Those who were twin-engine trained travelled to England by ship. The danger of such a journey was highlighted by the fact that a ship carrying some of their number was torpedoed in the Atlantic, however all on board were rescued.

On arrival in England, Peter underwent familiarisation training over the English countryside, again flying Oxfords. Then came a posting to an Australian operational unit at RAF Litchfield where he joined an all-Australian crew.

In 1943, Peter was flying Lancasters with the famous 460 Squadron. On 3rd and 4th April, the then Sergeant Coldham piloted Lancaster "G" for George in raids on Essen and Kiel. "G" for George now dominates the Aeroplane Hall at the Australian War Memorial in Canberra. After five operations with 460 Squadron, Peter transferred to the Pathfinders of 156 Squadron on Anzac Day 1943.

Of all the groups in the RAF, the Pathfinders had surely one of the most extraordinary roles. It was their task to lead bomber raids and drop target indicators to make the bombing more accurate and effective. Sometimes the Pathfinders would fly in ahead of the bombers and sometimes in mid-wave to re-mark targets for those still coming on to their targets. Peter recorded that much of the work was routine and a bit of a grind but there were times of great elation when flying over enemy targets. He described a real "high" when dodging searchlights and flak. It was during his time with Pathfinders that he was twice awarded the Distinguished Flying Cross, first in 1943 and the second time in 1944 for "great courage and determination" in the face of enemy opposition.

Peter had flown as a visual marker on raids over Hamburg which required the dropping of coloured target indicators on clear nights and on cloudy nights required the use of radar. In the raid on the rocket experimental and development base at Peenemunde, he dropped red spot fires on the island approach to the target, a task which required absolute precision and split-second timing. By the end of the war, he had flown six operations over Berlin. All told, Peter flew

46 operations in two tours of duty, the second of which he extended voluntarily in order to remain with his crew. It was time for Flight Lieutenant Coldham to think about returning to civilian life.

His first steps in post-war employment were not, however, back to the law. In 1945, he applied for a position in the Department of External Affairs, and after all the necessary interviews, was advised that he was soon to be appointed as an acting Second Secretary in the Department with the prospect of a posting to one of Australia's embassies. This was not, however, to happen. A medical examination revealed that Peter had tuberculosis and he spent much of the next year in hospital. By January 1946, he had fully recovered and, once again had an interview with External Affairs. The interview was followed by a protracted silence. Nothing happened for ages. He was eventually advised that his appointment as a Second Secretary had come through but it was then too late. He had decided to go to the Bar.

His Articles had been interrupted in 1941 when he joined the RAAF but he was able to resume with the firm of Krcrouse, Oldham and Darvall. Once his Articles were completed, he was admitted to practise and then, in February 1947, he signed the Bar Roll and embarked on the career he had contemplated as a small boy listening to barristers at work in the mid-1930s.

In his early years at the Bar, he did some criminal work and some Public Solicitor work and even turned his hand to a little prosecuting, but it was the common law work that was his first love and he was very good at it. His close friends at the Bar in those early days were Tony Murray, William Kaye and William Crockett, all of whom later sat on the bench of the Victorian Supreme Court.

The *Australian Law Journal* records that Peter "soon acquired a high and deserved reputation as a jury advocate". Many of his cases established legal "records". In one he obtained the highest damages at the time ever paid to a widow whose husband was killed in a factory incident. In another, *Richards v State of Victoria*, he obtained record damages of £69,000 for a boy who had been hit in the head at school and suffered permanent damage from a ruptured meningeal artery. The jury was out for seven hours but it returned its decision in favour of Peter's client.

After a short time at the Bar, Peter began to receive briefs in libel actions from the Herald and Weekly Times although it was not for them that he was a junior brief in the Royal Commission into Communist Activity in Victoria in 1949. He appeared for Cecil Sharpley who had been an organizer for the Communist Party of Australia and who had been in hiding throughout the Royal Commission's hearings and never moved without a bodyguard. After the hearings, Sharpley went back to England but Peter received Christmas cards from him for many years thereafter.

In 1960, Peter was involved in the inquiry into the crash of a Fokker Friendship at Mackay and in 1962 in the inquiry into the crash of a Viscount into Botany Bay. He also assisted in the coronial inquiry into the Southern Aurora train crash.

He was appointed Queen's Counsel in 1963.

In 1966, Peter was appointed Deputy President of the Courts Martial Appeal Tribunal which led to the hearing of a number of cases relating to serious offences committed by members of the armed forces, including two appeals by soldiers who had been convicted by Court Martial of murdering officers in Vietnam.

Peter's reputation as a fine barrister and capable administrator led to a term on the Victorian Bar Council from 1967 and later as its Chairman from 1969 to 1971 and membership of the Executive of the Law Council of Australia in the same years.

Although he declined the appointment at first, he decided to become a Presidential Member of the Commonwealth Conciliation and Arbitration Commission in February 1971. It meant a complete career change as he had never appeared in an industrial case before his appointment to the bench. He was now the Honourable Mr Justice Coldham, Deputy President of the Commission and also the Flight Crew Officers Industrial Tribunal. Accepting the appointments was a decision he never regretted.

The significance of the work done by the industrial bench is not widely appreciated. Peter soon learnt how important to the whole community are the decisions made by such a body. Many of the cases which came before the Commission were routine but some had immense impact. He was a member of the bench which prescribed equal pay for male and female employees performing work of equal value. Peter presided in annual leave cases and the very significant maternity leave case. In the appeals division, he presided over the case which brought teaching into the industrial jurisdiction. He was several times taken to the High Court by way of prerogative writs of prohibition, certiorari and mandamus, the nature of which requires the matters to be recorded as *R v Coldham*, the traditional citation used in criminal matters. He trusted that future students will not be misled into thinking that he embarked on a career of crime, by way of light relief, during his years on the bench!

He considered his most extraordinary case to be one which centred on occupational health and safety in the vehicle industry. The industry decided that it should have its own award and, after twelve months, it was affirmed by the Commission. Its decision demonstrated the enormous power of the Commission in that it effectively over-rode the legislation of five State parliaments.

The Honourable Mr Justice Coldham retired as Deputy President of the Australian Conciliation and Arbitration Commission in February 1989 but this was not to be a long retirement. On 1st March, he became Acting Deputy President of the newly-formed Industrial Relations Commission and remained in that post until his "real" retirement in August of that year.

Amongst a life-time of varied and challenging work, Peter considered that his work as Chairman of the Committee of Reference for Defence Forces Pay was the most interesting.

At one time, he sat with another distinguished Caulfield Grammarian, Air Marshal Sir Alister Murdoch, who had been Chief of the Air Staff. This was no "board room" committee; its task was to deal with issues of equal pay in the armed services; to fix pay scales for Reserve Forces; and to determine pay for submariners. Peter and his committee gained first-hand understanding of their work by spending 18 hours under the ocean in a Royal Australian Navy submarine. It was quite an experience. Thousands of people were on the beach when Peter and Sir Alister were piped aboard a navy launch which sped them to the waiting submarine. He recalled that, on other occasions, he and his committee members were winched into helicopters and aboard ships and did a great deal of travelling and inspecting in order to ensure that their decisions were as informed as possible.

Peter admitted to only one regret. Whilst at the University of Melbourne, he played district cricket. He gave it away at the age of 20 because of pressure of examinations. His regret was that he did not go back to playing serious cricket after the war, although he did play for some years with the Caulfield Grammarians. He led an exciting and interesting life. He was a brave and distinguished airman and, as a barrister and judge, left behind a reputation for high competence and skill in the many areas of law in which he worked.

Bill Sayers

1927 – 2007

Bill Sayers came to Caulfield as a pupil in 1938, having won a St Mary's Church Choir Scholarship, followed later by a Government Junior Scholarship. Over the next seven years, he involved himself in nearly every aspect of school life, rising to positions of leadership in Davies House and in the Cadet Unit where he became a Cadet Lieutenant in his final year.

Aside from being a sound student, he competed in almost every house sport and debated for Davies House and was awarded House Colours. He was also a member of the First XVIII and the School Athletics Team and appeared in two school plays. When, in his last year as a student, he told his headmaster, Frank Archer, of his interest in pursuing a career in teaching, he was strongly encouraged to follow that path.

In 1945, having completed his secondary education, Bill returned to Caulfield as a trainee teacher with specific involvement in the boarding house. That appointment led to a career connexion with the school which lasted over 50 years.

Bill taught at what is now known as Caulfield Campus until 1963 and, during that time, was a resident master, form teacher of various classes (most notably at Year 8), teacher of English and, on occasions, of French. He led the Scout Troop for five years and continued his involvement in the

Cadet Unit which he commanded until 1970, retiring with the rank of Major and having been awarded the Cadet Forces Medal and clasp.

He had the happy knack of choosing the right staff members to be Officers of Cadets and identifying the right students to pursue leadership roles in the unit. He managed, in his stride, the extraordinary logistics of the annual Cadet Camp at Puckapunyal and was frequently commended for the way the unit turned out.

One of the highlights of Bill's time in command of the unit was the mounting of the Honour Guard to greet the Governor, Sir Dallas Brooks, when he opened the Memorial Hall in 1958. Another highlight was the Passing Out Parade in 1963 when the inspecting officer was Air Vice-Marshal Douglas Candy, Deputy Chief of the Air Staff and a former student of the school.

When the Cadet Unit was disbanded in the early 1980s, it was Bill who was invited to hand over the Cadet Unit Colours which are now laid up in the Chapel of St Paul at Caulfield Campus.

Maintaining his interest in theatre and music, Bill was heavily involved in the Theatre Guild, directing eight school plays and appearing as Dr Sparling in R.C. Sheriff's *Home at Seven*, the first production in the newly built Memorial Hall in 1958 and performed entirely by members of staff. He was also involved in the production of *Bullumbimbi*, a musical written by Anthony Kitton and Bill Callander and music by

Norman Kaye, with its cast of 68 students from the senior and junior school.

Bill did me a huge favour in 1960 when theatre director George Fairfax was looking for a boy to play a role at the Melbourne Little Theatre (later St Martin's Theatre) in Jean Anouilh's *Traveller Without Luggage*. Bill nominated me for the role and that began for me a short but fun career as an actor.

At the end of 1962, Bill was invited by the then headmaster, Stan Kurrle, to take up the post of Master-in-Charge at Malvern Memorial Grammar School and to manage its affiliation with Caulfield. This he achieved with great care and tact, culminating in the smooth amalgamation of the two schools.

Anxious to ensure the strongest possible links between Malvern and the "senior school", Bill made every endeavour to combine activities in music and choir with the assistance of Norman Kaye and in sport with the help of Geoff Wilkinson and Jack Leahy.

During his time at Malvern, Bill sought the building of the swimming pool and the tennis court and the re-modelling of the science room and creation of the library, all achieved with the approval of the National Trust and the Historic Buildings Council which had more than a passing interest in the main building. Bill took his love of theatre and music to Malvern and many will remember his involvement with staff and students in performances of *H.M.S. Pinafore*, *Oliver!* and *Trial by Jury*.

Although he had not been a member of the Scout Association for many years, he had supported the 15th Malvern Scout Group as part of his nurturing of community welfare activities. The Association awarded him its Thanks Badge in 1983.

In 1965, Bill drew together a group of men who dedicated themselves to assisting the development of the school's outdoor education centre at Yarra Junction. This group, the Y.J. Fathers' Group, has continued to support Yarra Junction to the present day. Back in 1946, Bill had been involved in the demolition of an old army hut at Braybrook which was then transported and re-erected at Yarra Junction.

Ever mindful of the world beyond the school gate, Bill and Keith Grundy of Pulteney Grammar School in Adelaide developed an annual exchange between Malvern and Pulteney which became a multi-school sports and cultural exchange programme.

At the end of 1984, Bill took leave of Malvern Campus (as it was known by then) and, in 1985, became the school's Executive Director of Community Affairs until he retired in 1990. During those five years, he managed the affairs of the Caulfield Grammarians' Association with great skill and developed strong links with the various auxiliaries and support groups connected with the school. His work paved the way for girls to be part of the Association from 1986 onwards. He worked closely with the then Development Officer, to establish a formal data base to keep alive connexions with former students and involve them in matters such as providing career advice and work experience for current students. This has been a great help to those who have followed Bill in the role.

He returned to Malvern for the last time in 2005 when the drawing room was named the Bill Sayers Room and an early portrait of him was put on permanent display.

Although generally a robust character, Bill suffered a stroke in 1967 from which he seemed to recover but which may have been the underlying cause of ill health which plagued him in his later years. He died on 21st January 2007, survived by his wife, Ann, and their four children. He is remembered as a wise, able, generous and caring man.

John Morrison

1904 – 1998

In 1989, Her Majesty the Queen appointed John Morrison a Member of the Order of Australia for service to Australian literature. John was neither a student nor a teacher at Caulfield but he came to us as a gardener in the 1930s and early 1940s, returning in 1950 and staying until 1963 with most people completely unaware that one of the country's most distinguished writers was in their midst.

John was born in 1904 in Sunderland, England, and arrived in Australia in 1923. He had left school at 14 and went to work as assistant to the curator of Sunderland Public Museum and Winter Gardens where he had the run of the library.

After a couple of years there, he was employed as a trainee gardener for a wealthy ship owner in East Boldon.

His first Australian job was in the garden of the historic Zara Station at Wanganella near Deniliquin. He returned briefly to England in 1927 but came back Australia the following year, spending the next ten years as a wharf labourer.

Initially contributing stories to trade union magazines and also to *Meanjin*, his first collection of short stories, *Sailors Belong Ships*, was published in 1947 and was followed by *The Creeping City* in 1949, *Port of Call* in 1950 and *Black Cargo* in 1955. *Twenty-three* followed in 1962, *Selected Stories* in 1972, *Australian by Choice* in 1973, *North Wind* in 1982, *Stories of the Waterfront* in 1984, *This Freedom* in 1985 and *The Happy Warrior* in 1987.

John's stories of the industrial conflicts on Melbourne's waterfront are still of interest as is his portrait of the impact of football on domestic life in the story "Black Night in Collingwood". At last count, his stories have been published in more than ten languages, including Russian, Chinese and Italian and many feature in anthologies.

The December 1947 issue of the school magazine records: "Mr John Morrison, formerly on the school staff as gardener, is steadily achieving a reputation as one of Australia's most promising writers. A volume of his stories has just been published by the Dolphin Press under the title *Sailors Belong Ships*, and shortly his first novel with an Australian setting will appear. Mr Morrison was recently awarded a Fellowship under the Commonwealth Government Literary Fund. We express our pleasure at his success and our good wishes for future projects". He was awarded another such Fellowship in 1949.

John received the gold medal of the Australian Literature Society in 1963 and the Patrick White Literary Award in 1986. He also held an Emeritus Fellowship granted by the Australia Council. In 1974, the Victorian branch of the Fellowship of Australian Writers instituted the John Morrison Short Story Award.

After leaving Caulfield, John became a full-time writer producing five more collections of short stories and his memoirs but there were no more mentions in the school magazine.

John's socialist convictions were always reflected in his choice of characters and the situations in which they found themselves. Although his range of stories is wide, his attitude is consistent and is revealed implicitly as a belief in the simple virtues of work, loyalty and self-discipline, illustrated in life as he cared for the garden at Caulfield.

High praise has been given him. Stephen Murray-Smith believed that "Pioneer", one of the stories in *North Wind*, is the finest story written in Australia since Henry Lawson. Alan Marshall said of John that "no native-born reflects the spirit of Australia more than he does".

In 2003, a caricature portrait of John by Noel Counihan was presented to the Common Room at Caulfield Campus to mark his contribution to Australian literature.

George Sproule

1889 – 1976

George Moore Sproule was born on 8th August 1889 at Highton near Geelong. His father later became vicar of St Clement's Church at the corner of Brighton Road and Glen Huntly Road in Elsternwick and it was from the vicarage that young George travelled to Caulfield Grammar School at the age of eight. He was pupil number 622 on the school roll.

The Speech Day Report for 1897 gives us the first glimpse that George was no ordinary schoolboy. He was Dux of Form IIIb in that year and, in 1898, followed that up as Dux of IIIa. On 19th December 1900 he collected a special prize for excellence in mathematics, history, geography and physiology. Two years later, the Speech Day Report records that, on 31st October, he had run third in the one mile race in the Annual Sports held at the St Kilda Cricket Ground. At the end of the year, he was placed first in Latin and French, first in mathematics and was mid-winter and Christmas Dux of IVa.

In 1903, George was in Vb, Sub-Matriculation, and managed a second place in history, geography and physiology and third place in mathematics. In athletics, he was placed second in the 440 yards (Junior Cup) and second in the Open Mile. The following year saw him win the one mile race at the Annual Sports and run second in the Under 16 200 yards. He was also placed first in English and second in algebra. 1905 was an outstanding year for George as he passed Matriculation in English, Latin, Greek, history, physiology, geometry, algebra and with honours in French. He was placed second in the open mile in the Schools' Championship of Victoria which, overall, was won by Caulfield against all public and private schools in the state. In addition to that success, George had a particularly successful day at the Annual Sports in October, being placed third in the 120 yards, second in the 300 yards, first in the egg and spoon race which, for senior boys, must have been run as a novelty event, and he came second in the mile. The Speech Day Report for 1906 noted his Trinity College Exhibition and his pass in the Senior Public Honour Examination in mathematics. His sporting achievements were equally impressive: third in the open 440, first in the open 880 and second in the open mile in the Secondary Schools' Championship, in which Caulfield was placed second. He was also the winner of the school's goal kicking competition in football.

His career at Caulfield demonstrated the very balance of sporting and academic achievements which made it possible for him to be viewed so favourably by the Rhodes Scholarship selection panel just five years later.

Headmaster W.M. Buntine said of George that he "was always a careful, conscientious student, possessed of unusually good intellectual ability, and one who set about his studies with a manly definiteness and purpose. His record for classwork, extending as it does over nine years of school life, is exceptionally good. He stands out as one of the best students on the school register. As an athlete, the record of G.M. Sproule is almost as striking as the record of his achievement in class work. When quite a little fellow, he exhibited unusual qualities of determination and self-control and gave promise of the distinguished career he was afterwards to have. At the age of ten he attracted attention of all one Sports Day by the pluck and endurance he showed in the attempt to win the mile walk. Amongst his school fellows Sproule was always deservedly popular, and exerted a quiet, personal influence which was of the best and highest kind. His character was transparently honest, both in relation to his class mates and to his masters, by all of whom he was highly esteemed".

Called upon to serve as referees for his Rhodes Scholarship application in 1910, members of staff J.S. Taylor, Arthur Astley, R.W. McCulloch, G.H. Easton and Frank Archer all endorsed Buntine's comments by saying that "all along Sproule has conducted himself with marked ability and honour, both in form and field, gaining the affection and respect of his school fellows and a high place in the esteem of his masters. On all occasions when in the upper school he used his influence for good. And showed readiness to lead whenever opportunity offered".

George began reading for the degree of Bachelor of Arts at the University of Melbourne in 1907, becoming a resident of Trinity College in order to take up the Warden's exhibition he had received in 1906. At the end of 1907 he passed all compulsory subjects, obtaining honours in deductive logic. In his second year at Melbourne he secured First Class Honours in inductive logic and mental philosophy as well as turning his hand to rowing. He gained a seat in the University Novice Fours regatta and his crew finished in second place.

1909 was a vintage year for him in both his studies and his sport. He passed third year Arts and first year Education as well as the practical tests for registration as a primary and secondary teacher. In addition to participating in University Union debates, he ran first in the half mile, first in the mile and first in the two mile at the University Annual Sports. He was placed third in the Five Mile Teams Race and was the fastest novice without a handicap. In the VAAA Three Mile Victorian Trial he ran first and was selected for the interstate team to compete in the one and three mile events in Brisbane at the Australian Amateur Championships. He also ran second for the university in the five mile cross country and third in the ten mile.

In his final year, George again distinguished himself in study and games. He took out First Class Final Honours in the School of Logic and Philosophy, thus gaining the Hastie Final Honour Scholarship, funded from the estate of John Hastie of Corangamite who had left his money and property to the Church of England, the Presbyterian Church and to the university. Aside from finding time to graduate as a Bachelor of Arts, George ran second in the University Championship Mile, first in the Two Mile University Handicap, from the back mark, and first in the one mile in the Inter-Varsity Sports in Sydney. He was awarded a Full Blue for his outstanding achievements in athletics.

The School Magazine of 16th June 1910 records George's

appointment to the staff of Caulfield Grammar School and indicates that the new third form were very proud of their new master. Given that it was the age of hero worship, George, with all his talents and achievements must have seemed god-like to his young charges. Later in the year, the headmaster tells us that George "has had the sole charge of 23 little boys, whose ages range from 11 to 13 years, in all their subjects and has secured excellent results with them. With the natural gift for putting things before the boys in a pleasant and interesting way, he has shown sympathy with them and has very speedily gained their entire confidence. Rarely has a boy in his form to be checked for conduct, for there is a manifest desire to attend and to please rather than displease the teacher". High praise indeed for a man only months after starting as a teacher.

George continued to teach at Caulfield into 1911. The School Magazine of November 1911 tells us that a send-off was given for him at the school on 21st August, following his selection as the Victorian Rhodes Scholar for 1911. A travelling bag and silver inkstand were presented to him by the masters and boys. He made a brief speech of thanks which was followed by sustained applause for a noticeably long time. A couple of days later, he sailed for England and Balliol College, Oxford.

Reading through the testimonials provided in support of George's application, it is plainly evident that these qualities were observed in him by some of the most eminent Melburnians of the day. Dr Alexander Leeper, Warden of Trinity, attested that George had outstanding talents and "a special gift for the study of Philosophy, and to be exceptionally fitted to derive the fullest benefit from life at Oxford and from an honours course in the studies for which that University is still chiefly famous . . . I should with great confidence predict that Mr Sproule . . . will take a First Class in Greats and I believe that there is also a strong probability that he will win a Fellowship. I have never had a student (not even Mr Behan) about whom I could have made such a forecast with more confidence".

It did not take long for George to make his mark at Oxford as an athlete. The newspaper *The Sportsman* of 6th November 1911 reported that "the Varsity Hare and Hounds Club opened the season on Saturday with a Novices and Freshmen's Race . . . the club has a promising recruit in Sproule, a newly arrived Rhodes Scholar, who brings with him the Five-mile Championship of Victoria". His performance in this event was reported in the *Daily Mirror* in London which went on to say, "Unfortunately, owing to a mishap to the official watch, no times were taken".

The following week's issue of *The Varsity* reports that George ran against Surrey Athletic Club in a five-mile event and that "Sproule worked up into third place in the second two miles. Sproule's effort was quite unexpected, and though it would be unsafe to prophesy so early in the season, will probably turn out a cross-country runner of a very high order". He was placed second on this occasion.

Virtually every issue of *The Varsity* from 1911 to 1914 carries some report of George's exploits in cross-country running.

In February 1912 he competed in the Southern Counties Cross-Country Championship and, by running in 52nd place, helped Oxford to fourth position. Some 260 runners competed.

His career as an athlete was not forgotten at home for an unidentified Australian newspaper cutting dated 17th April 1912 reminds the selectors of the Australian Olympic team to compete in Stockholm in July that George is living in England and will be available for the team. The cutting is interesting for more than the news of George; the reverse reports the sinking of the *Titanic*!

George won the 'A' Team v Oxford Harriers event in March 1912 and put up a fine performance to win the 7½ mile event against Thames Hare and Hounds in November. *The Varsity* records that "the Shotover course appears to be getting shorter each week . . . the starters were faced with a bitterly cold wind, but Moore set out to make the running at a tremendous pace, and continued it to the foot of the hill: we doubt whether anyone has ever led the field with such graceful skill and speeds. Sproule passed him going up Shotover and kept in front, finishing in 39 min. 24 sec."

In January 1913, George competed in the annual cross-country event between Oxford and Cambridge, again at Roehampton over 7½ miles. The Varsity reported that "the day was not exactly an ideal one for racing, for a strong wind was blowing and the course was heavy, there being more plough than last year, though the brooks were not running so strongly . . . Sproule's time (44 minutes 13 seconds) was some 30 seconds slower than that of the winner last year". In addition to honours in his academic work, he was awarded medals for the Oxford v Cambridge three-mile event and the OUAC three-mile and one-mile events, being placed third, second and third respectively.

His final year at Oxford began with yet more success in the cross-country field reported in *The Varsity*. Covering the Oxford v Cambridge event of the previous December, it indicated that George's winning time of 41 minutes 55 seconds was a new record for the race, even though the Oxford team was beaten by Cambridge by three points. George's fame as an athlete was not overlooked: "Leaving the run put up by Allan in the three-mile Victorian Championship, we come to an even more brilliant performance, namely that credited to Geo. M. Sproule, the Victorian Rhodes Scholar, this week in London when he covered the three miles in 14 min. 34 sec., creating a new University record. Only a few weeks previous to this he was timed to do the distance in 14 min. 52 sec. Sproule's latest run is well inside Australasian figures (14 min. 49 sec.) standing to the credit of the late W. Simpson (NZ). With youth on his side, the young Australian should have many years ahead of him on the track and across country. Like J.L. Davis and several other brilliant Victorian athletes, he was formerly a student at Caulfield Grammar School". For both of these three-mile runs he was awarded University medals.

The *Oxford University Gazette* of 10th August 1914 announced that George Moore Sproule had been admitted to the degree of Bachelor of Arts. He had capped off a distinguished academic career with the *Literae Humaniores aegrotat* and now his second BA. Who can tell what academic career he would have carved out for himself had not the guns of August already begun their rumblings in Europe. On the day he graduated, the Great War was six days old.

Like many of his contemporaries at Oxford, George responded to the call to arms. *The Sketch* of 31st March 1915 listed him among the 76 of the 127 Oxford Blues of 1914 who had "joined the colours". He was commissioned as a Second Lieutenant in the Army Service Corps on 31st August 1914, just three weeks after war had been declared. He was posted to the 11th Divisional Train as adjutant and from there to the 26th Divisional Train. This posting took him to one of the lesser known battle zones of the war, Salonika.

In a desperate effort to aid the retreating Serbs in October 1915, the Allies sent an expeditionary force of 185,000 men to Salonika, despite the fact that Greece was a neutral country and that political agreement for the action had not as yet been reached. The British and French then advanced into Serbia to try to link up with the Serbs, but a combination of foul weather and skilful action by the Bulgars drove them back to Salonika, where they proceeded to construct a huge entrenched camp. The British contingent was commanded by Lieutenant-General Sir Bryan Mahon who, 15 years earlier, had led the flying column which had relieved Mafeking.

The Salonika campaign was a disaster. On military grounds, the evacuation of Salonika was indicated but political considerations induced the Allies to remain. The Dardanelles failure had already cost the Allies dearly in prestige so the Salonika force was augmented with a view to checking German influence over Greece and maintaining a base of operation from which to aid Rumania if, as expected, it entered the war on the Allies' side. With gentle sarcasm the Germans described Salonika as "the greatest internment camp in the world" into which the Allies had withdrawn and bolted the door behind themselves. As adjutant to the Divisional Train, George was kept extremely busy. It was during his stay in Salonika that he was twice Mentioned in Dispatches and, in November 1917, he was awarded the Military Cross. He was invalided home to England on 8th December 1917 but he was fit enough seven months later to be attached to the Royal Dublin Fusiliers, serving in France, Belgium, Greek Macedonia, Serbia, Bulgaria, European Turkey and the islands of the Aegean. He remained in France until December 1918, taking up teaching again as an educational officer with the 17th Division. This task was devised to keep the soldiers busy until they were repatriated home.

During one of his short spells of leave in 1918, George found the time to marry Eithne Lennox Magee, a member of the Irish Players with the Abbey Theatre, Dublin. Like many military brides, Eithne had to fit her domestic life around the requirements of army service.

After the Great War, George continued to serve with the Royal Army Service Corps, first as the Corps's adjutant in

London from 1919 to 1921 and then with the Rhine Army Train, again as adjutant from 1921 until 1923. In recognition of his work in war and peace, he was elected to Membership of the Institute of Mechanical Engineers in 1926.

Family life was not, however, totally subjugated to the demands of military service. In 1920, a son was born to Captain and Mrs Sproule and he was named George Denis. Their first daughter, Eithne Mary (Wendy) was born in Cologne, Germany, in 1922 whilst her father was serving with the Rhine Army. Their younger daughter, Patricia Ann (Paddy), was born in Middlesex in 1924.

In 1927, George went to the War Office as Inspector of Mechanical Transport and remained in that post until 1931 when he became an instructor at the Army Technical School in Chepstow, being promoted to the rank of Major in 1932. On the restoration of Corps establishment in 1934, he commanded 42 Company at Aldershot until taking up the appointment as instructor at the RASC Training Centre in November 1935. In 1936, he took on the additional role of editor of *The Journal of the Royal Army Service Corps*. His Golden Jubilee issue is still considered one of the finest examples of a commemorative military journal.

After an extremely interesting career spanning 25 years with the RASC, George retired on 4th March 1939, to take charge of the London office of the newly constituted Herring Industry Board, but this was not to be a long engagement. Events in Europe were to draw him back into uniform before the year was out.

The Second World War began on 3rd September 1939 and George was recalled to the RASC on 24th October and assigned to the Department of the Quartermaster-General to the Forces as Deputy Assistant Director of Salvage, being promoted Lieutenant-Colonel in 1941. He also took responsibility for the maintenance of RASC records and remained in that post until he was retired from the army on medical grounds at the end of the war in 1945. His son had been killed in action with the RAF in 1941 and the loss had affected him deeply. In addition, the shell shock he had suffered in the Great War was beginning to take its toll.

George returned to the Herring Industry Board when he left the army but, again, his stay was short. He became Principal of the Employment Department in the London Chamber of Commerce in 1946, retiring from that post in 1954 at the age of 65. From 1954 to 1958, he worked for the army at Aldershot as a Retired Officer.

In 1958, George and his wife moved to make their home by the sea at Ferring in Sussex on the south coast. He occupied himself with rug-making while he watched sport, particularly track and field, on television. Despite his leaving the army on medical grounds, his health remained sound during his retirement and his mind always alert. Like most ex-servicemen, he maintained an interest in politics; his views were mainly right wing, pro-Empire and disposed against Britain entering the Common Market. Family and friends gathered at Ferring on 18th January 1968 to help George and Eithne celebrate their golden wedding anniversary.

George never returned to Australia. His service in the regular army made it difficult for him to find the time and opportunity to visit. Two of his sisters had followed him to live in England so he did not feel cut off from his family. By the time travelling became faster and easier and he was more free, he felt he was too old to cope with the journey. His younger daughter, Paddy, tried unsuccessfully to persuade him to go with her on a trip to Melbourne in 1974 and he was very envious of her visit to his old school.

Eithne died in 1975 and George was completely shattered. His health began to deteriorate rapidly and he died only 14 months later on 25th July 1976.

Both of his grandsons completed the London Marathon but, sadly, George did not live to see them do so. He took a great interest in their running achievements at Rugby School, as he did with all activities of the young with whom he was always immensely popular. He would have been very proud indeed to have seen his younger grandson wearing his original 1914 Oxford University running shorts and singlet in the 1982 London Marathon. He did, however, live to see man land on the moon which he had, from their early days, told his children would happen in his lifetime.

Alan Sumner

1911 – 1994

Until relatively recently, Caulfield owned only two significant works of art. One was Noel Counihan's splendid portrait of Gemmell Lamb Smith and the other was Alan Sumner's huge stained glass window installed in the foyer of the Memorial Hall in 1958.

Alan was neither a student nor a teacher at Caulfield but his great window is the one thing of beauty that no student at the school since 1958 could ever forget. It is such a magnificent and complex work that I would not dare attempt a description save to say that it honours all Grammarians who have lost their lives in war, hence its name – Sacrifice.

Alan was born in Northcote in 1911 and was educated at Collingwood Technical College and at RMIT. He went on to study at the National Gallery School and studied under George Bell who was a leader of the modern art movement in Victoria. He also studied printmaking in collaboration with John Rule. Alan specialised in silk screen prints and stained glass, winning the Crouch Prize in 1948. From 1954 to 1968, he was head of the National Gallery School in Melbourne.

Caulfield commissioned him to create the window for the Memorial Hall but Alan had been unwell so it was not in place until after the opening by the Governor on 27th April, 1958. The window was a gift from the boys of that year who raised the £800 by a very strange process. Each was provided with books of small tear-off "tickets" which were sold to family, friends, neighbours and unsuspecting strangers. So far, it sounds like a raffle but there was no prize! Out of the goodness of their hearts, people paid a few shillings for tickets and the boys handed in the money and the stubs.

Over the years, the window suffered minor damage. A golf ball or two and even a football or two broke small pieces of glass. Many boys will remember the portly figure of Alan, high on a ladder, effecting repairs.

On the morning of Melbourne Cup Day in 2000, I was wakened by a telephone call from one of the boarders, Luke Boland, who rather breathlessly informed me that the Memorial Hall had burnt down during the night. I jumped out of bed and raced to school to see the shockingly burnt shell of the hall but, to my absolute amazement, the window did not seem badly damaged. I had expected to find it a pile of coloured glass scattered on the ground; it had sagged at the bottom but it was largely intact.

Only a few weeks earlier, Luke and I had climbed (quite illegally) to the top of the building so he could take panoramic photographs. Now there was no top. It was a blackened creature with its bones sticking up in the air. Luke and I just stood and looked; neither of us could say anything.

I discovered later that the fire chief had played water on the window all night and it had been saved, almost the only thing to survive the fire. Fortunately, most of the treasures which could be removed had been taken out prior to the commencement of the renovations which were almost complete when the fire broke out. Sadly, we lost the magnificent Fincham pipe organ which could never be replaced.

The contract for the restoration of the window was given to Ferguson Glass in Glen Waverley. Students and teachers watched as each panel was carefully removed and taken away. Principal Stephen Newton and I visited Ferguson Glass where we were given a very pleasant surprise.

When Alan Sumner died, Ferguson Glass had purchased his entire stock of coloured glass from his estate so the damage to our window was repaired using the same glass stock that Alan had used to create it 42 years earlier. When the rebuilt Memorial Hall (now the Cripps Centre) was completed, Alan's window was back in place and continues to remind us of why it was first commissioned.

Alan had solo exhibitions in Ballarat, Melbourne, Sydney and Brisbane and is represented in the Australian National Gallery in Canberra, in all State galleries, Ballarat Art Gallery and in Australian Government Embassy Collections. Other of Alan's large windows can be seen in St Brigid's Church in Mordialloc.

Her Majesty the Queen appointed Alan a Member of the Order of the British Empire for service to Australian art in 1978.

Bruce Lumsden

1917 – 2004

Bruce Lumsden was born in Melbourne and grew up in an evangelical environment. His father was a missionary and his mother ran a hostel in Prahran for the Melbourne Bible Institute.

As a student in his final year at Caulfield in 1935, he was a Prefect, house vice-captain, leader of the Crusader Union, Captain of the First XVIII, Captain of Athletics and equal Dux of the school. He spent a year at the Melbourne Bible Institute after completing a Bachelor of Arts degree at the University of Melbourne and then accepted a post at South Melbourne Technical School.

When war broke out, Bruce was accepted by the RAAF for aircrew training and then went to England for further training for massed bomber raids on Germany. After 20 day and night raids over Europe, Flight Lieutenant Lumsden was an observer in a Lancaster A4H flying in daylight on 2nd November 1944 to bomb a synthetic oil refinery on the Rhine near Duisberg. Operating in formation for the first time, things went wrong from the start, culminating in the squadron commander's aircraft developing trouble, which required Bruce's pilot to take the lead – only to have the rest of the squadron fall behind.

Flying alone, they reached their target and dropped their bombs, but their aircraft was struck several times by enemy fire and the crew had to bale out behind enemy lines. Bruce was taken prisoner almost immediately. He was transported across Germany and spent some time in Dulag Luft before being imprisoned in the notorious Stalag Luft III at Sagan until he was marched to Stalag IIIA at Luckenwalde, near Berlin, ahead of the advancing Soviet army.

Arriving ill and exhausted, Bruce found conditions worse than experienced at Sagan. There was no hot water nor any provision for washing. On 22nd April 1945, the prisoners awoke to find their guards had disappeared. Later in the morning, Russian troops entered the camp but it wasn't until 20th May that the Red Army agreed to hand over the British and American POWs to the Americans. Bruce eventually reached England and, a few weeks later, sailed for Australia.

Working for the Scripture Union in Sydney after he was released from the RAAF, he renewed friendship with Honor Moss, a nursing sister at the Anzac Memorial Hospital in Katoomba. They were engaged in 1946 and married in January 1947, a week before Bruce joined the staff at Caulfield.

He remained at Caulfield for eight years and, in that time, completed a Diploma in Education. He coached the First XVIII and taught all but the top levels. In January 1955, he took up the post of General Secretary of the Scripture Union in New Zealand and returned to Sydney after eight years to fill the same role for the Australian office. In 1965, he became the sixth headmaster of Caulfield Grammar School.

Bruce led Caulfield through exciting and very challenging times. He fostered a stimulating environment of creative learning and imaginative teaching that led the way in the independent school sector. In all of this, he was aided greatly by a very able staff which included Bill Callander (who became his deputy in 1971), Ken Barret, Don Wirth and John Nelson. New subjects, teaching methods and administrative structures were trialled. A political forum was created and the arts flourished.

All of this was happening against a background of the Vietnam War and its aftermath, with dissent at all levels. Bruce did not favour the response of repression, preferring to create and maintain an environment in which individuals were encouraged to play a role in the management of the school. He knew this would not be easy, but said, "If our real concern is to achieve real and fruitful relationships with the youth of an age of rapid change rather than preserve every existing cherished institution intact – and this seems to me sometimes to be the dilemma – we may have to be willing to shed some of our prejudices and personal tastes". His approach did not sit well with everyone.

After he retired from Caulfield in 1977, Bruce became a part-time consultant with the Commonwealth Schools Commission and, for nine years, was a member of the Victorian Planning and Finance Committee, which was set up to assist disadvantaged country schools with funds for essential capital works. For 15 years after his retirement from Caulfield, he served as a voluntary community tutor, working with students with learning difficulties. His life was one of service to its very end.

Toby (a horse)

floruit **1945 – 1955**

The horse's body is a fine example of nature's ability to relate structure to function. It is adapted for speed and size. Toby was not fast but he was certainly big. He was a Clydesdale, a draught horse, and had been acquired by the school to draw the mower gangs which cut the grass on the oval.

In horse-speak, Toby stood slightly over 16 hands with heavy fetlocks. His near side fore cannon was white as were his hind cannons and he had a wide blaze. In other words, he was taller than your average racehorse and had strong ankles. His front left leg had a white sock as did both back legs and the front of his face was also white. The rest of his coat was dark brown.

He was a very placid horse and boys loved him. They were not supposed to feed him but quite a few mothers (mine included) might have wondered why lunch bags had pieces of carrot or sugar cubes added to them. The curator, Alf Mills, took great care of Toby and few boys were allowed to ride him. In the archives is a splendid photograph of a young boarder, Ian Murphy, in his full school uniform and cap happily perched on Toby's back. Ian came from an equestrian background and Alf knew he could be trusted.

Sometimes, however, it was Toby who couldn't be trusted. He was an escapologist and, on occasions, usually at night, managed to get out of his enclosure and go wandering. Alf would receive a telephone call from a neighbour or the police asking him to retrieve Toby from a front garden where he was happily snacking, or from Greenmeadows Gardens, a small park not far from the school.

Toby also had an acute sense of smell. In those days, boys took their lunch to school in brown paper bags and Toby often sensed something truly delicious in a bag or two left on the edge of the oval while their owners were busy at kick-to-kick out in the middle. This was about the only time Toby moved quickly – and the lunches were gone.

I suppose we can call it progress but poor Toby suffered the ignominy of being replaced by a second-hand Ferguson tractor. We all missed him and I am sure he missed us too.

Don Barrett

1917 – 1973

When we think of past-student politicians, the name of Don Barrett does not automatically spring to mind. It should. Don was instrumental in the development of parliamentary government in Papua New Guinea.

He was born in Adelaide in 1917, the son of distinguished writer Charles Barrett who also wrote under the name of Donald Barr. Don came to Caulfield as a five year-old in 1923 and, as he progressed through the primary and secondary years, he was recognized as a more than capable student. Both his mother and father became involved in the embryonic Parents' Association and, over the years, donated a large number of books to the school library as well as contributing to the Memorial Hall fund.

In 1934, School House awarded him House Colours and he was appointed a Probationer Prefect. In his final year, he was a School Prefect, Captain of School House and ended the year as Dux of School. The December issue of *The Caulfield Grammarian* noted that he possessed an excellent collection of Australian and Empire postage stamps.

In 1936, he began reading for the degree of Bachelor of Commerce at the University of Melbourne but maintained a close connexion with his school as a committee member of the Caulfield Grammarians Association. In fact, he was instrumental in the formation of the Younger Caulfield Grammarians Association. Don's report in the December 1937 issue of the school magazine records a year of interesting and varied activities conducted by the YCGA and the promise that "all boys leaving school this year (will be) assured of a hearty welcome . . . when the first annual general meeting will be held, followed by a mock Speech Night".

Don had always been an organizer. In his first year out of school, he formed a committee of prefects from the previous four years. He called it the Old Prefects Scheme and its aim was to assist the school in a host of ways, from working bees to mentoring. He also served on the committee of the Old Grammarians Football Club.

Don completed his studies in 1940. With the war a year old, he joined the army and received a commission. By 1942, he was a Captain and had topped a course for artillerymen in Sydney. A posting to the 1st Armoured Division took him to New Guinea which turned out to be fortuitous.

A training cadre of Australian officers and warrant officers, together with a few volunteers from the Royal Papuan Constabulary, assumed the responsibility of turning into soldiers a group of Orokaiva men from near Kokoda who had been recruited. This was the genesis of what was to become the Pacific Islands Regiment. Don was the original adjutant of the 2nd New Guinea Infantry Battalion and served with the unit through its raising, training and action until he moved to Headquarters PIR after the end of the war.

Don finished his service with the rank of Major but he chose not to return to live in Australia. Perhaps developing from his father's interest in nature and the environment and his own "nature study" exhibits which were a feature of the Hobbies Exhibitions at school, he decided to become a planter. He grew cocoa and coffee as well as producing copra on his plantation at Vunakanau. He became President of the Plantation Association and a member of the Producers' Control Board. His property was about 12 miles from Rabaul and his house was built on a site used by the Japanese as an anti-aircraft gun emplacement. It had a great view of Blanche Bay and a steaming volcano!

From 1949 to 1957, Don was an elected member of the first PNG Legislative Council. He was chosen as one of the ten representatives of the territory to come to Canberra in 1953 to meet Queen Elizabeth. The following year, he made another brief return to Australia and ensured that Caulfield was on his itinerary, He spoke at a school assembly about his life and work in PNG.

Don was elected to the Legislative Council again from 1960 to 1964 when he was elected to the Council's successor, the House of Assembly. He held the seat of West Gazelle until 1967.

He was a man who exuded confidence. He always believed he was needed and the best man for the job. He generally was. He was never still, always planning, pushing, working, talking. The Melanesian Tourist Federation was beginning to take wing under his leadership. Just before he died, he was planning to go to Guam to see if he could bring forward the date of the next South Pacific Games. He had been an organizer of the Games in Port Moresby in 1969 and had been actively involved in all of the Games which followed.

He will be best remembered as a New Guinea politician who always did his homework, whose constructive criticism from the floor of the House was devastating in its accuracy, and who was one of the pioneers of parliamentary democracy in PNG.

Sir Alister Murdoch

1912 – 1984

Alister Murdoch was born in Melbourne on 9th December 1912 and, at the age of ten, entered Caulfield Grammar School. His family lived close by in a magnificent house at 10 Orrong Road. (It is worth a look!) Alister made an impression on the school right from the start. In 1923, he was top in arithmetic, mental arithmetic, English and writing. The following year, he won the Ernest Morgan Prize, awarded to the boy in Form IVb who had shown most aptitude and diligence. His talents were not confined to the classroom and he soon demonstrated his abilities as a sprinter and tennis player.

Over the next four years, he maintained a high academic standard, won prizes in athletics and was awarded Colours by Barnett House.

His final year at Caulfield was an extremely busy one. He was a member of the tennis and football premiership teams. He was beaten only once in the inter-school tennis season and was awarded School Colours for tennis. His membership of the Barnett House Committee gave him the opportunity to demonstrate his ability to organize and to lead. At the end of the year, Alister and classmate Douglas Candy were selected by the Defence Department to be trained in the Air Force Wing of the Royal Military College, Duntroon. It is interesting to note that Candy went on to reach the rank of Air Vice-Marshal and was Air Member for Personnel. Murdoch left Caulfield with academic and sporting awards and a reputation as a quiet achiever.

Alister and Doug Candy were two of the first four cadets to be selected for officer training by the RAAF. At Duntroon, Alister entered into the curriculum in the right spirit and quickly established himself as a leader in academic studies and in sport. He had a quiet manner and approached all problems with cold logic; he needed no extravagant gestures to make his point. Training at Duntroon went on smoothly until events were affected by the depression of 1930. For economic reasons, the Army Board decided to move officer training from Canberra to Victoria Barracks in Sydney where, owing to restricted accommodation, the RAAF cadets could not be taken. Consequently, after two years instead of the normal four years' training, Alister was posted to Point Cook in January 1931 to undergo pilot training. He received his wings in December of that year and was commissioned a Pilot Officer on 1st January 1932. He then went on the first of a series of specialist training courses, starting with an introduction to seaplanes. He flew Moths fitted with floats, the Mark 1 Seagull, the old wooden-hulled aircraft, and the twin-engined Southampton flying boat.

It was as a result of this specialist training on seaplanes that Alister was selected for a most unusual assignment. On November 23 1935, the American explorer Lincoln Ellsworth and his English pilot Herbert Hollick-Kenyon lost contact with their base whilst attempting a trans-continental flight across Antarctica in his Northrop Gamma aircraft "Polar Star". Sir Hubert Wilkins, aboard Ellsworth's ship *Wyatt Earp*, heard Ellsworth's last radio signal, "Still Clear; no wind . . ." then silence. He raised the alarm and, on 23rd December, *Discovery II* sailed heavily laden from Williamstown. There did not appear to be one inch of deck space not taken up with fuel and various supplies.

Among the ship's company were two RAAF officers: Flight Lieutenant Eric Douglas, who had flown the plane Mawson had carried south in the *Discovery II* in 1929, and Alister Murdoch. They took with them a Gipsy Moth seaplane, which they planned to use for short reconnaissance and observation flights, and a Westland Wapiti, a bomber and larger plane, planned for use in the main rescue. As it turned out, the Wapiti was never used.

Ellsworth and Hollick-Kenyon were, in fact, quite safe. They had landed in soft snow and were out of fuel so they set off on foot, intending to reach Little America. They reached it on 15th December and, finding a skylight in what had been Admiral Richard Byrd's radio shack, climbed down and settled in to await the arrival of the *Wyatt Earp*.

On 15th January 1936, whilst Ellsworth was asleep, Hollick-Kenyon heard an aeroplane overhead and rushed out in time to see a parachute hit the ground. It had a parcel of supplies attached to it and a note from the captain of the RSS *Discovery II* asking them to go to the shore to meet a party of his men. The plane was the Gipsy Moth with Eric Douglas and Alister aboard.

Years later, Alister said that flying in a "whiteout" with the primitive instruments of the time was a most frightening experience. Simple things like starting the Moth's engine posed major problems. They built a stove under the Moth's nose with a chimney leading up to the engine to keep it warm.

Before they left Little America, Eric Douglas and Alister went on an airman's pilgrimage on their skis to the remains of the "Blue Blade", the wrecked Fokker monoplane left by Admiral Byrd. One wing of it pointed skyward through the snow about a quarter of a mile away.

On his return to Australia, Alister played down this extraordinary adventure and treated the whole episode as if it had been a pleasant holiday trip to Tasmania. He soon settled back to work and completed a flying instructor's course and was engaged in those duties until he went to the United Kingdom late in 1936 to do the "N" Course, the Long Navigation Course at RAF Manston.

Several RAAF officers were on board the RMS *Strathnaver* and they did not take long to notice the attention Alister was paying to a very attractive girl passenger called "Bobbie" Miller. They were married at the end of 1937 and spent their honeymoon in Switzerland.

After Alister had completed the "N" Course, he was attached to 114 Squadron to gain some experience on Blenheim aircraft. On his return to Australia in 1938, he was posted to RAAF Headquarters in the Operations and Intelligence Branch. At the outbreak of war in 1939, he opened the Air Observers' School at Cootamundra but, very soon after, he was attached to the RAF. He was given a Wellington bomber squadron fitted with an early form of radar. The squadron moved from Northern Ireland to Iceland and then to the Middle East, all in a period of some five weeks. They then joined a wing in a forward area of the desert but were pushed back to El Alamein.

Alister was then posted back to London to the staff of Lord Mountbatten where he became involved in the combined operations raid on Dieppe. Fortunately, the destroyer in which he was travelling was not hit by anything larger than small shells. His comment on the raid was that every dive bomber seemed to be aiming directly at him.

He returned to Australia late in 1942 as Senior Air Staff Officer Eastern Area from 1943 to 1944 and Northern Area until 1945, based in Darwin. May 1945 found him Chief of Operations on Morotai Island with the 1st Tactical Air Force commanded by Frederick Scherger. It was here that Operation OBOE began which was to take the allies progressively to control of Tarakan, Labuan and Balikpapan. Alister said that "it would never be forgotten that the real background behind OBOE was the recovery of British occupied or administered territory. It was for the Americans to spear northwards to areas from which they had been previously evicted by the Japanese, and for the British and Australian forces to go into Borneo, especially where the British had been so entrenched. It was a matter of national morale that these areas be recovered". They were. As a result of his work on Operation OBOE, Alister was appointed a Commander of the Order of the British Empire by King George VI in 1946.

In September 1945, Alister returned to Air Force Headquarters, Melbourne, as Director of Postings and he became Director of Personnel Services in October 1946. He attended a staff course at the Imperial Defence College, London, in October 1947 before re-joining Air Force Headquarters as Director of

Air Staff Plans from 1949 to 1952. Promoted to Air Commodore and appointed Commandant, RAAF College, Point Cook, in 1952, the next year he became Air Officer Commanding, Training Command Headquarters, Melbourne.

The RAAF's anticipation of 'new look' equipment, especially in fighters and transports, was spurred initially by the findings of an investigating team led by Alister which, in 1954, concluded that the Lockheed company's developing F-104 Starfighter and its new C-130 Hercules transport were most suited to the RAAF's needs. Ultimately, the Hercules, the Orion maritime aircraft and the De Havilland Vampire were acquired.

Seconded to the Department of Defence as Deputy Secretary (Military) in January 1956, Alister became Air Vice-Marshal in 1957 and was appointed Deputy Chief of the Air Staff in February 1958. He went to London the following year to head the Australian Joint Services Staff. Appointed a Companion of the Order of the Bath in 1960, Alister returned to Australia in 1962 to lead Operational Command. Promoted to Air Marshal and made Chief of the Air Staff in June 1965, he was knighted a year later.

Alister led the RAAF at the time of its biggest peacetime expansion, when it moved from subsonic to supersonic aircraft. He saw the Mirage fighter come into service and witnessed radical changes in approaches to maintenance and cleanliness which were essential for effective supersonic operations. In order to increase surveillance of the Indian and Pacific oceans, Alister transferred the Orion's base from

Townsville, Queensland, to Edinburgh, South Australia. He also oversaw the introduction of the F111, which was to become the RAAF's principal strike craft. Interested in upgrading training facilities, he established a new school for radio mechanics at Laverton, Victoria, to bring the service into the electronic era.

A calm leader, Alister avoided involvement in political issues and did not scheme in any way. Having developed a good working relationship with the Americans, he achieved the unusual distinction of getting along with most people while making tough strategic and administrative decisions. He worked effectively with his ministers, the government providing the RAAF with sufficient resources to make it the highly efficient force that it was at the time of the Vietnam War. During his term as Chief of the Air Staff, however, there was some criticism of the RAAF's perceived failure to fully assist the army. Despite the fact that Iroquois helicopters had been acquired primarily to support the army, he refused the Chief of the General Staff's request to send two of them to Vietnam to provide support because he doubted it would be a valuable experience. To be fair, the army did little to encourage what was supposed to be a co-operative function.

A keen golfer and racegoer, the pipe-smoking Alister retired from the RAAF on 31 December 1969. He joined a committee, headed by another Caulfield Grammarian, Justice Peter Coldham, to consider the pay scales of all three services and in 1981 he became chairman of Meggitt Ltd, a company developing electronics and aerospace equipment.

Survived by his wife and their daughter, Alister died on 24 October 1984 at Mona Vale, Sydney. Described by Sir Frederick Scherger as 'the last of the professionals', Alister was a quiet, private man who wanted no parade or ceremony to mark his passing.

Ric Hawkins

1947 -1967

In early February 1967, the news slowly filtered through to the leavers of 1964 that one of their best and brightest was dead. Richard Charles Hawkins had been severely injured in a motor vehicle collision in Bambra Road, Caulfield, on 6th February and died at the Alfred Hospital two days later. He was 19 years old.

Born in 1947, Ric arrived at Caulfield in 1959, joining Buntine House. He soon demonstrated that he was confident, articulate and witty, all qualities he would put to use over the next six years.

He would never have described himself as a gun sportsman but he was always willing to have a go. In Year 9, he volunteered to run in the ¾ mile for Buntine House and came a valiant third. By the time he reached Year 12 in 1964, he had represented his House in swimming, debating, chess and athletics.

Academically, Ric was sound, passing eight Intermediate

and six Leaving subjects, but it was on the stage that the school saw just how talented he really was. The Theatre Guild staged "Play Night 63" and Ric starred in *The Valiant* as Warden Holt, an officer toughened by years of prison experience, working with the prison chaplain in an attempt to save a prisoner condemned to death.

In House debating, Ric helped raise Buntine to the highest place in the competition for many years. Tall, lightly built, head tilted slightly to one side and with an engaging smile, he presented his arguments with precision, often leavened with humour, and was a master of rebuttal.

Another of his talents came to the fore when, in Year 11, he exhibited four caricature portraits of members of the teaching staff. As portraits they were incredibly accurate but as caricatures they were amazing. His drawing of history master Harold Pennefather illustrated Harold's quirky dress but still brought out all the warmth of his personality. It hung in the Harold Pennefather Reading Room in the library for many years but is now in the school archives.

In Year 12, Ric joined the School A3 Debating team and was a participant in "Parliament of Youth" on Channel 7 on the topic "Is a war worth winning?" Three members of the Open Debating Team were "ministers" and 12 were "backbenchers".

Again, with the Theatre Guild, Ric played the king in "Night with Shakespeare", an extract from *Hamlet* complete with hair-raising duels and bloody murder.

In the winter of 1964, Ric played football as a member of

the 5th XVIII, otherwise known as the "Gentlemen's XVIII". His tongue-in-cheek report on the season's performance published in *The Caulfield Grammarian* is a gem: "The team commenced the 1964 season with a unique win against Scotch. Our score was cancelled in the third quarter for having 19 men on the field – a true illustration of our team spirit – but we were able to fight on to win comfortably . . . Although we only won one out of five matches, when we did win we acted as if we were used to it and when we lost, we acted as though we were only doing it for a pleasant change".

Possibly the best demonstration of his writing skill was his "School Diary (with a difference) 1964" which began the School Notes section of the magazine of that year. If you can track down a copy of the magazine, it will reward your search. I have lost count of the number of times I have read it and it never ceases to amuse – even if he does falsely accuse me of stealing half the second speaker's case in the "Parliament of Youth" debate! His illustrations appear with the article and in other places in the magazine.

Ric finished the year well, fulfilling all the requirements to pass Matriculation and gain entry to Monash University's arts faculty, planning to major in history for his arts degree. He had also applied for law but did not receive an early offer so he returned to Caulfield for a second Year 12, not uncommon in those days. He was appointed a prefect and settled to work but a late law offer arrived and he was off to Clayton. Aside from study in his two years at Monash, he buzzed around on his motorbike and threw himself into undergraduate life with some of the more exotic and activist characters who were there at the time.

On the evening of 6th February 1967, Ric dressed up, left his parents' home in Hawthorn Road, Caulfield, jumped on his motorbike and took off.

About 7.35 pm, Fire Brigade Officers responded to an activated street fire alarm (such free-standing alarms don't exist today) at the corner of Bambra Road and Eskdale Road in Caulfield. They found a motorbike lying on the footpath about four feet away from the damaged street alarm on the south-west corner of the intersection. A Holden sedan was parked about seven or eight feet away from the motorbike.

Ric was lying on the footpath against a fence in Bambra Road. The occupants of the Holden were standing near their car. One of the firemen radioed for the police and ambulance to attend. Just as he put the radio down, the motorbike burst into flames; it was quickly put out. The other fireman assisted Ric as best he could.

While they were waiting for the police and ambulance to arrive, a middle-aged man approached one of the firemen and said, "I am a witness to the accident. I was following the motor cycle along Bambra Road before the crash. We were going at a moderate speed. The Holden was coming down Bambra Road towards us when it did a right-hand turn in front of him and cut him off".

The man gave his name to the fireman as R. Brooksby. He stayed for a little while but then said he had to leave. He told the fireman that he would report to the Caulfield Police Station in the morning. He did not report to the police and was never subsequently located. The firemen said that they did not see his car.

Ric was taken to the Alfred Hospital and the police interviewed the driver and her husband, both of whom said they saw nothing until the motorbike hit their car. Asked if she had her car lights on, the driver said the lights were not on and it was not dark. It was, however, dusk as this was four years before daylight saving. The police report stated that the Holden appeared to have cut the corner while turning and there were no skid marks. The driver denied that she had cut the corner.

The injuries Ric sustained were catastrophic and he died two days later.

Coroner Pascoe conducted an inquest into Ric's death. He had statements from the emergency services personnel and the doctor who issued the death certificate. In the absence of a statement from the mysterious R. Brooksby, Mr Pascoe concluded his finding by saying, "The evidence adduced does not enable me to determine the direction of travel of the deceased or whether the death was accidental or otherwise". Sadly, we shall never know what really happened.

With his death, we lost a wonderful and multi-talented friend. He is buried in the Brighton Cemetery, near where I live. I visit him sometimes.

Tom Stock

1877 – 1900

If you had walked into the old Memorial Hall, half way up the right-hand stairs to the auditorium and had a look over your right shoulder, you would have seen a marble memorial plaque in memory of Private Thomas Stock. It was a gift to the school from his classmates following his death in South Africa.

Tom was a boarder at Caulfield from 1893 to 1896. He came from Sandford in rural Victoria but we know little about him as a schoolboy as there was no school magazine recording boys' exploits and no other evidence of his performance at school exists.

When Tom and his brother, Duncan, volunteered to go to South Africa to fight the Boers, they were not raw recruits. Whilst farming at Sandford, they had been for over two years members of the Casterton Mounted Rifles. They went to South Africa with the 1st Victorian (Mounted Infantry) Contingent at the beginning of the war, arriving in Cape Town on 26th November, 1899. As soon as the horses had recovered their land legs, the contingent moved via the Orange River to Belmont as an advance guard for the Australian infantry. By mid-December, Tom was near Modder River where heavy fighting ensued throughout January and early February when Tom was sent on picket duty at Hobkirk's farm near Pink Hill. On 12th February, the Boers attacked at dawn and continued the attack until mid-afternoon. Of the 18 men involved, Tom and eight others were killed.

Initially, word came to the Stock family in Australia that Duncan had been killed. On 3rd March, a burial party went out to find bodies. They located four who could be identified but one, shot through the head, had no identity card although a silver watch, missed by the Boers, was found in his pocket and a few days later Duncan identified it as belonging to Tom. Unaware of the confusion of identities, Duncan sent the sad news of his brother's death to his family.

Tom was buried at Kloof Camp in Cape Province but, in 1905, the bodies were exhumed and re-interred in the military cemetery at Colesberg on 14th February 1906 with full military honours provided by the 3rd Battalion of the Royal Fusiliers, including an escort of 100 men and a band.

Duncan did his best to shield the family from the reality of Tom's death. There is an undated newspaper cutting in the school archives which refers to a letter from Duncan. In it he says, "The Boers wounded most of our horse-holders and when our men had to retire the fire was so hot on the horses they thought it better to let them go and foot it back to camp. They had a hard fight . . . Poor Tom got shot in the breast while making a hard fight to get away, and dropped dead. The ambulance men got him all right." Duncan survived the Boer War, served in the Great War and lived in Casterton until his death on 23rd January 1949 at the age of 84.

Such was the reaction to Tom's death at Caulfield, a ceremony was held on Friday 27th July 1900 at which the marble plaque given by his school fellows was unveiled. In attendance were past and present students, parents, staff and friends. Malcolm MacKenzie, MP, chaired the ceremony and speeches were made by him, by past students, by a war correspondent who had been with Tom at Pink Hill and by the Headmaster, Walter Buntine, who said, "It seems almost impossible that one of the boys of the school who would be best remembered by his prominence in all school concerns, his cheerful nature and his boyish love of sport, in which he distinguished himself in contest with school teams, could, in little more than three years, have found a soldier's grave on the African veldt. Men appear as they are, in a crisis. Tom was always an earnest boy possessed by a strong determination. He was a generous boy who was ever ready to make allowance for the faults of others, and had won for himself a very strong attachment by his school fellows. The Old Boys have done a wise thing in perpetuating his memory in the manner in which they have, for boys are natural hero worshippers, and the boys of Caulfield Grammar School have in Tom Stock a worthy hero".

Other memorials to Tom can be found in the Anglican Church at Sandford, at the South African Fallen Soldiers Memorial in Casterton, at the Boer War Memorial in Hamilton, the South African War Memorial in Ballarat and at the Central Memorial in Bloemfontein Cemetery in South Africa. A cypress tree was planted in his memory at the gates of the Casterton Hospital. Since the re-building of the Memorial Hall, the Caulfield plaque has been kept in the school archives.

Lindsay Thompson

1923 – 2008

Often described as "the gentleman of Australian politics", Lindsay Thompson was born on 15th October 1923 at Warburton. His father, Arthur Thompson, had studied theology in Sydney but enlisted in the AIF when the Great War broke out. Becoming seriously ill, Arthur was discharged from the army but, recovering sufficiently, he became a teacher and later made an unsuccessful attempt to enter Federal Parliament for the National Labour Party in the seat of Maribyrnong.

Lindsay's mother, Ethel May, was also a school teacher with a passionate interest in Australian politics and international affairs.

After the death of her husband in 1928, Ethel Thompson moved her family from Glen Iris to Elsternwick to live with her sister and her family.

In 1929, Lindsay became a pupil at Caulfield Grammar School where he was placed in the charge of two older boys who showed the newcomer the bounds of the school. One of those boys grew up to become Professor Peter Karmel, Chairman of the Australian Universities Commission, and the other the Reverend Stanley Kurrle, Headmaster of Caulfield Grammar School and subsequently The King's School in Sydney.

Lindsay was an outstanding student, sportsman and leader.

He was Dux of School in 1940. In 1941, he became Captain of Buntine House, Captain of School and Captain of the First XI. He played football with the First XVIII, debated for Buntine and was awarded House Colours for cricket, football, athletics, tennis and debating. He was also on the staff of the student newspaper, *News and Views*, and *The Caulfield Grammarian*.

By the time he finished school, the Second World War was well under way. While waiting for a call from the army, Lindsay spent ten weeks of 1942 as a resident master at Caulfield and thoroughly enjoyed the experience.

On 14th April 1942, Lindsay reported for army duty at Caulfield Racecourse and from there to Bendigo and the Signals Training Battalion. By October 1943, he was in Port Moresby where he was attached to New Guinea Force Headquarters. He returned to Australia in April 1945, suffering from persistent attacks of malaria.

Although still unwell, Lindsay commenced an honours history and political science course at the University of Melbourne in 1946. Attacks of malaria continued and he was admitted to Heidelberg Repatriation Hospital where he was treated with the new anti-malaria drug, paludrine. A stint working on a cousin's farm at Waikato in New Zealand, in combination with the medication, returned him to health. He came back to Australia in 1947 to resume his course.

It was at university that Lindsay gained his first taste of politics, winning election to the Student Representative

Council on a ticket committed to wrest control from the communists and socialists who had dominated it for some years. In 1948, the SRC successfully confronted the Tramways Union by running a bus service from Flinders Street Station to the university during a tram strike.

In January 1950, Lindsay married Joan Poynder, whom he had first met in 1945 while on a fortnight's holiday at Lorne on Victoria's south coast. They had become engaged in 1948 and had decided to marry after Lindsay's final examinations in November 1949.

Lindsay gained his teaching qualification in December 1950 and was posted to Spring Road Central School in Malvern. In 1953, he transferred to Melbourne Boys' High School, where the principal was George Langley, who served with the Camel Corps in the Great War, and the vice-principal was the former Australian cricket captain, William Woodfull.

During his first year at Melbourne Boys' High School, Lindsay unsuccessfully sought pre-selection for the Legislative Assembly seat of Malvern.

At the end of 1954, the headmastership of Caulfield Grammar School was to become vacant with the retirement of Frank Archer. Lindsay applied for the post and was one of two short-listed candidates interviewed by the selection committee on 7th September 1953. The third and chosen candidate was Stanley Kurrle who was then a curate in England and who had been one of Lindsay's guides when he started at Caulfield in 1929.

In July 1954, illness again intervened and Lindsay spent some weeks in hospital recovering from a number of operations and a post-operative infection. When he recovered, he attempted pre-selection in three new seats, created by a redistribution of boundaries. Again he was unsuccessful but, a month later, the death of a sitting member created a vacancy in the Legislative Council Province of Higinbotham. This time, Lindsay was successful. He threw himself into a six-week campaign and, on 19th April 1955, he took his seat in the Legislative Council at the age of 31.

This was the time of the split in the Australian Labor Party. Matters came to a head on Lindsay's first day in parliament. The next day proved to be the last day of the Cain Labor Government. Elections were held in May, installing a Liberal Country Party Government under Henry Bolte with a majority of one.

In 1956, Lindsay became parliamentary secretary to Cabinet. In July 1958, he was sworn in as a minister and given the roles of Assistant Chief Secretary and Assistant Attorney-General. Holding Cabinet office from 1958 until his retirement from Parliament in 1982 gave him a record term as a Victorian Cabinet Minister.

During his time as Assistant Chief Secretary, Lindsay came into contact with Dr John Birrell who had been appointed Police Surgeon in 1957. By travelling with Dr Birrell or with members of the Accident Appreciation Squad, Lindsay gained a first-hand understanding of Victoria's high road toll which led to the introduction of the breathalyser and the .05 blood alcohol limit for drivers. Later, in 1970, Lindsay was responsible for Victoria being the first jurisdiction in the world to legislate for the compulsory wearing of seat belts in motor vehicles.

In 1960, Lindsay became Assistant Minister for Transport. After the general election in 1961 and a cabinet re-shuffle, he became Minister for Housing and Forests. The portfolio of Aboriginal Welfare was added in 1965. As Housing Minister, Lindsay played a significant role in promoting home ownership and encouraged the sale of Housing Commission houses to their occupiers.

The retirement of John Bloomfield as Education Minister in 1967 saw Lindsay transfer to that portfolio which he was to hold until 1979. He had also transferred to the Legislative Council seat of Monash in 1967.

His time as Education Minister was one of considerable unrest among teachers and saw militant activity by the Victorian Secondary Teachers' Association. Lindsay was obliged to cope with union unrest; a shortage of good teachers, especially at secondary level; a monolithic and inefficient education bureaucracy; and a history of low expenditure on education stretching back to the 1920s.

All of these issues were addressed during his twelve years as Minister, leaving Victorian education in good shape when the portfolio was handed to his successor.

It was during his time as Education Minister that Lindsay, in 1970, resigned his seat in the Legislative Council and won the seat of Malvern in the Legislative Assembly.

Two years later, Lindsay was to become involved in an extraordinary event. In September 1972, two men kidnapped six small girls and their teacher, Mary Gibbs, from the Faraday school near Castlemaine. They had left a note on a school desk, addressed to Lindsay as Education Minister, demanding $1 million. Early the next morning, Lindsay received a telephone message to bring the money to the Woodend Post Office at 5.00 a.m.

Lindsay stood in the pre-dawn with the bag of money. A man drove by several times but no-one approached. By sunrise, it was clear that the kidnappers would not appear. Soon a message came through that the Faraday seven were safe. Mary Gibbs had kicked a panel out of the back of the van in which she and the children were being held and had led them out. Rabbiters took them to the Lancefield Police Station. For her bravery, Mary Gibbs was awarded the George Medal. Lindsay received the bronze medal of the Royal Humane Society.

In May 1979, Lindsay transferred to the Treasury portfolio. At the same time, he was sworn in as Minister for Police and Emergency Services and held that office for two years. He had long been concerned about Commonwealth-State financial relations and the need for Victoria to press for a more equitable deal from the Commonwealth. He sought a fairer tax-sharing arrangement and persisted in his demands for the remainder of his time in the Victorian Parliament.

Henry Bolte had been succeeded by Rupert Hamer as Premier in 1972 and Lindsay had then become Deputy Premier. Much innovation had occurred during Hamer's premiership but, by 1981, he was being openly criticised by his party colleagues. Matters came to a head and Hamer resigned at the end of May, leaving Lindsay as Acting Premier.

In the party room on 2nd June, Lindsay was elected to lead the Liberal Party with his rival, Bill Borthwick, elected as his deputy.

On 3rd April 1982, John Cain Jnr ended 27 years of conservative government in Victoria. Lindsay remained briefly as Leader of the Opposition but retired from Parliament on 5th November 1982. In addition to being the longest serving Cabinet Minister, he was the longest serving member of the Victorian Parliament and the longest serving Education Minister.

As well as his parliamentary role, Lindsay was, at various times, Deputy Chairman of the Australian Advertising Standards Council, Chairman of the English Speaking Union Scholarship Committee, Chairman of the National Tennis Centre, Premier Patron of the Richmond Football Club (where his son, Murray, was a player), Committee Member and Chairman of the Melbourne Cricket Ground Trust and the Australian Gallery of Sport, President of the Victorian Lifesaving Society and President of the Victorian Parliamentary Former Members Association. In all of these fields, he served with rare decency, dedication and distinction.

In 1975, Her Majesty the Queen appointed Lindsay a Companion of the Order of St Michael and St George and, in 1990, an Officer of the Order of Australia.

Throughout his life, Lindsay maintained a high level of interest in his old school and all of its activities. It was the school to which he sent his sons and his grandchildren followed. He was the keynote speaker at the school's Centenary Dinner in 1981 and he and Joan were present in November 1997 when the sports centre was named in his honour. Without any fuss, he would arrive at matches being played at school, find a comfortable seat and enjoy the company of anyone who chose to pass the afternoon with him.

Barry Patten

1927 – 2003

Having lived in Melbourne most of my life, I am reasonably familiar with the city's great buildings. On a number of occasions, I have had cause to visit the state government's offices in Macarthur Street. I have enjoyed concerts, ballet performances and Carols by Candlelight at the Sidney Myer Music Bowl and, since my retirement from Caulfield, I have travelled past 140 William Street on the tram as I head towards my office near the County Court. It never crossed my mind that those buildings could have been designed by the same architect or that he might have been a Caulfield Grammarian.

They were and he was!

Barry Patten hit the ground running when he arrived at Caulfield in 1941, joining class D1, School House and 4 platoon in the cadet unit. He passed Intermediate in six subjects. The following year saw him on the First XVIII practice list, promoted to corporal in the cadet unit and walking off with the Tom Rowe Shield for his model aeroplanes shown at the annual Hobbies Exhibition. He won the Under16 100 yards at the House Sports and, in the Associated Grammar Schools Combined Sports, ran sixth in the 100 yards and ran the first leg for the 440 relay team which came second. He scored three goals in the First XVIII game against Trinity Grammar School and was named best on ground. At the end of the year, he qualified for promotion to sergeant in the cadet unit and passed Leaving.

In 1943, his last year at Caulfield, he was awarded House Colours for football, athletics and swimming and won the Open Mile at the House Sports and ran seventh in that event in the AGS Combined Sports.

Barry studied architecture at the Melbourne Technical College and, in 1948, transferred into fourth year architecture at the University of Melbourne. At the same time as he was finalising his studies, he trained hard as an alpine skier, becoming national champion and winning selection in the Australian Olympic Team to compete in Oslo in 1952, unfortunately missing out on the medal rounds. He also took up surf lifesaving, winning the State Beach Sprint Championship in 1949.

Following his graduation, Barry joined the firm of Yuncken Freeman Brothers, Griffiths and Simpson and, in 1957, submitted a wire and paper model design for the Sidney Myer Music Bowl which was successful. It was only six years since he had graduated as an architect. The building celebrated its 60th anniversary in 2019.

In 1966, Barry's design for the State Government Offices was chosen because of its sensitivity to the history of the area as it was to be built in close proximity to Parliament House and the Treasury Building. It was also to be built off the line of Collins Street which was an unusual response, given Melbourne's grid layout. The building was completed in 1969 and, in 1970, Yuncken Freeman won the Royal Australian Institute of Architects bronze medal for the design.

As the government offices were being completed, Barry was working on a design for BHP House at 140 William Street. When completed in 1972, it was the tallest building in Melbourne and the first building in Australia to generate its own electricity supply, from BHP natural gas. The use of steel and concrete, leading to open floor plates was innovative and became a standard feature of high-rise office buildings.

In 1968, Yuncken Freeman accepted the commission to build a high-rise apartment block in Toorak. Barry and his family built a large penthouse apartment atop the building and enjoyed sweeping views for the next three decades.

Barry left Yuncken Freeman in 1985 and joined a group of architects he had known since they were all students. The collaboration only lasted four years but they won an award for their refurbishment of the Savoy Plaza Hotel.

Like many professionals, Barry never really retired. He worked from home on a variety of projects involving conversions of office blocks and apartment buildings. He was, for a while, on the council of the Victorian Chapter of the RAIA and spent whatever time he could on his property in the Goulburn Valley where he bred Simmental cattle, a Swiss variety grown for both milk and meat. He died on 13th March 2003.

Michael Clyne

1939 - 2010

Michael Clyne's parents fled Vienna in 1938 as refugees from Nazism after the Anschluss. Michael was born in Melbourne the following year and came to Caulfield in 1950, joining Archer House. By 1953, he had cemented himself into the School Orchestra and can be seen gnome-like in his thick glasses, seated behind his cello in the photograph in *The Caulfield Grammarian*. There he remained for the next few years.

By 1956, he had passed nine Intermediate subjects and seven Leaving subjects. His team won the House Debating Cup in 1956 and Michael was also a member of the School Debating Team. He was an Open Day organizer and one of the group which edited *The Caulfield Grammarian*.

He passed Matriculation with First Class Honours in German and Second Class Honours in Economics, netting him a Commonwealth Scholarship. In his senior years at Caulfield, he had been influenced by another refugee from Nazism, Dr Samuel Billigheimer, who taught German and was a man of high culture.

Michael went on to the University of Melbourne where he completed a Bachelor of Arts degree and later a Master of Arts degree in linguistics. The Old Boys Notes in the 1957 school magazine, reporting on students at the university, quipped that Michael was learning so many foreign languages that he had entirely forgotten how to speak English.

In 1962, he joined the brand new Faculty of Arts at Monash University as a tutor in German and went on to become the university's first Doctor of Philosophy in that faculty.

Michael spent more than 40 years at Monash until his retirement as Professor of Linguistics in 2005. During that time, he was also a visiting professor at the Universities of Hamburg, Heidelberg, Stuttgart and Verona. He was the author, co-author or editor of 30 books and had written over 300 articles on linguistics.

In 1977, Michael married Irene Donoghue and they had one daughter, Joanna. Brian Porter and Kate Burridge's obituary for Michael in the *Sydney Morning Herald* tells of Michael and Irene's resolve that Michael would only speak with Joanna in German and Irene only in English – a good recipe for bilingualism.

Michael was the Chairman of the Monash Centre of Migrant Studies from 1974 to 1976 and again in 1985 and 1986; Vice-President of the Association of German Speaking Communities from 1979 to 1983; editor of the *Journal of Intercultural Studies* from 1977 to 1986; a member of the Ministerial Advisory Committee on Migrant and Multicultural Education from 1983 to 1987; a member of the Archbishop of Melbourne's Commission on Multicultural Ministry in 1985 and 1986; and the Diocesan Liturgical Committee from 1987 until the mid-1990s.

Recognizing his academic brilliance and his contribution to education, many honours came his way. He was appointed a Member of the Order of Australia in 1993 and, in 1996, he received the Austrian Cross of Honour (First Class). The German Cross of Merit was awarded in 2003, the year in which he received the Australian Centenary Medal. He received an honorary Doctor of Philosophy degree from Munich University and was appointed a Fellow of the Academy of Social Sciences of Australia, a Fellow of the Australian Academy of Humanities and a Foreign Member of the Royal Netherlands Academy of Science.

Porter and Burridge also point out that "Clyne's radiant smile and relentless curiosity to know and befriend his many students made him a legendary character in and around the Robert Menzies Building that became his scene. Indeed, so popular was he that he was awarded the first Monash Vice-Chancellor's Medal for post-graduate supervision".

They quote the late Joshua Fishman, an American linguist

who specialised in the sociology of language who wrote: "I could write almost endlessly about Michael Clyne. He is one of the saints that God has placed here among ordinary mortals in order to enable us to follow his lead in doing good things for all and sundry".

That is exactly how I remember him.

Noel Counihan

1913 – 1986

Noel was born in South Melbourne but his home was not a happy one. His parents were constantly at loggerheads, often physically. Art historian Bernard Smith suggests that, for Noel, his mother became an archetypal image of injustice.

He attended the local state school and, in 1922, he won a scholarship and became a chorister at St Paul's Cathedral School. This came about after initial rejection and several changes of primary school as the family shifted house several times.

Five years in the cathedral choir provided him with little enjoyment and he was often in trouble for passing on smutty stories, laughing at inappropriate times and macabre practical jokes. When he thought a chorister had been unfairly punished, he scratched "A.M. a victim of injustice" on the school lavatory wall. It remained there for years.

The final crunch came when he led a strike over the right

of choristers to play games in the Fitzroy Gardens. More or less in disgrace, Noel left the cathedral school in 1928 and found his way to Caulfield Grammar School, once his mother overcame his father's objections to the scheme.

Because of frequent interruptions to his primary education and the nature of his schooling at the cathedral school in Jolimont, his academic start at Caulfield was poor. Geometry was not taught at the choir school and he had not done well in algebra.

On his very first day, he fell foul of Billy Morcom, his mathematics teacher, who, as far as Noel was concerned, may well have been talking in Swahili. Morcom heaped sarcasm on him and Noel responded by drawing a caricature of Morcom on the blackboard prior to the next class.

In one of Gemmell Lamb Smith's history classes, Noel was drawing faces in the margin of his notebook when he felt a hand on his shoulder. Lamb Smith bent over and said to Noel, "They're very good, very good indeed. Why don't you put some of your drawings in the Hobbies Exhibition?" Lamb Smith struck up a good relationship with Noel and was pleased to see more caricatures of Morcom in the exhibition.

Noel did well in history and English but his maths and science results were less successful. He enjoyed life at Caulfield and he played tennis well. His talent for drawing also attracted the attention of his geography teacher, Joe Florance. Noel's drawings headed the cricket and tennis notes in *The Caulfield Grammarian* in 1928 and 1929. Lamb Smith and

Florance encouraged Noel to think of a career in art and suggested that he should leave Caulfield and take classes at the National Gallery School. When he attempted to enrol, he was told that, at 15, he was too young. As with the choir school, he had to wait another year and filled those months working for his father's hosiery firm in Flinders Lane as a stock-room assistant but he was sacked for leading a protest over unpaid overtime. He was unemployed and homeless.

For the next few months, he slept on the floor at the Workers' Art Club and later in the rooms of the Communist Party which he joined in 1931.

The Caulfield Grammarian of July 1933 noted that Noel's cartoons in *The Argus* camera supplement were watched with interest by all who were at school with him. It recorded that he had held his first exhibition and seemed well started on a successful artistic career.

Throughout the 1930s, he was very active politically and he also found work as a caricaturist. In 1933, he held his first exhibition and this resulted in a weekly commission for *The Argus* in Melbourne and then for Sydney's *Bulletin*, *Table Talk* and other magazines. In the same year, he was involved in a demonstration in Brunswick against police suppression of street meetings. He was jailed as a result but his conviction was overturned on appeal.

In 1939, Noel went to New Zealand where he worked as a caricaturist for the *New Zealand Observer* but he was deported after less than a year for his anti-conscription activities. It was in New Zealand that he met and married Patricia Edwards, a high school teacher, who followed him home on his forced departure.

A bout of tuberculosis in 1940 was followed by an intense period of self-education in which Noel taught himself to paint. His political activities were not neglected and he spent much energy organizing artists to protest against the rising threat of fascism.

Although a communist, Noel supported the Allied cause and was anxious to do something practical in the national interest. With Harold Herbert and a group of other artists, he successfully lobbied General Sir Thomas Blamey to utilize artists more effectively in the war effort in camouflage, cartography and as official war artists.

In 1944, Noel went to the state coal mine at Wonthaggi to make drawings of miners at work because he believed they were making a great contribution to the war effort but were getting little recognition. Knowing of his political activities, the management would not let him go down into the mines so he appealed to the miners' union which threatened to stop work if he were not allowed to go down. That did the trick. Under very difficult conditions, he drew by the light of his lamp in all parts of the mine. This experience resulted in two of his most highly regarded paintings, *Miners Working in Wet Conditions* and *Miners Preparing a Shot*. The names may be prosaic but the pictures are magnificent images of 20th Century Australian industrial labour.

Noel returned to Caulfield in 1944 as a guest of the Art Club where he spoke about his work and provided advice to budding artists and commentary on model drawing exhibits by members of the club.

After the war, he was well established as a portrait caricaturist for a variety of newspapers and magazines, including *The Beam*, a trotting magazine edited by the author Frank Hardy. He left Australia in 1949 to live in England where he worked for the *Daily Mail* supplying caricatures of leading politicians and, for the *Radio Times*, of popular entertainers of the time. He returned to Australia in 1952 and, in the late 1950s, he completed series of caricatures of VFL champions and local and visiting wrestlers on the stadium circuit.

Noel was a council member of the Victorian Artists' Society from 1961 to 1963 and was president of the Print Council of Australia in the 1970s. He exhibited widely in Australia and in London, Warsaw, Copenhagen, Moscow and Leningrad. He was honoured by a semi-retrospective exhibition at the National Gallery of Victoria and the Commonwealth Art Gallery, London, in 1973. In 1983, on his 70th birthday, he was invited to exhibit his lino-cut, lithographic and etching prints produced between 1931 and 1981, again at the National Gallery of Victoria.

Noel died on 5th July, 1986. In 1991, an exhibition of his work entitled *Images of a Working Life*, was organised by the Broken Hill City Art Gallery and subsequently toured Australia.

The boy who left Caulfield to enrol at the National Gallery School in 1930 who had "never realised before that a man could devote his life to drawing and painting" secured a permanent place for himself among the greatest of Australian artists.

Sir Davis Hughes

1910 – 2003

In March 1959, the leader of the National Party in the New South Wales Parliament, Davis Hughes, was forced to resign the leadership when it was shown that he had lied to the parliament about having a Bachelor of Science degree. He had been the Member for Armidale from 1950 to 1953 and from 1956 but it looked like the 1959 revelation could end his political career.

Davis was born in 1910 in Launceston, Tasmania. The family lived in Sheffield but his mother wanted him to have a good education so Davis moved in with his grandmother and attended Launceston High School. He would not have been described as a committed student but he was a natural sportsman and involved himself in rowing, football and cricket.

On leaving school, he commenced a science course at the University of Tasmania but did not complete the course. He switched to teacher training and was appointed to a one-teacher school even though his training was not finished.

In 1932, Davis joined the staff of Devonport High School where, aside from teaching science and mathematics, he took the First XI to a premiership in the Devon Cricket Association and to second place in the State Premiership. At the end of 1934, he travelled south again to join The Friends School in Hobart where he taught physics and mathematics to the examination classes and initially coached the junior cricket team and the boys' tennis team. In the first half of 1936, he coached the senior boys' cricket and football teams.

Coming to Caulfield in mid-1936, Davis quickly established himself as a vigorous and popular teacher in the boarding house, in the classroom and on the sports field. He immersed himself in the life of a young resident master in School House. In addition to his teaching, he was appointed coach of the Second XVIII and made it very clear that he expected hard work at practice.

By 1937, he was vice-captain of the Old Caulfield Grammarians football team, a mainstay of the forward line who kicked 54 goals during the season, many with place kicks.

Davis played a role in a wide variety of school activities. He adjudicated debates, ran net practice for young cricketers and, in 1938, led a visit to Trinity Grammar School in Sydney with Caulfield cricketers, athletes and debaters. For the Hobbies Concert, he directed A.A. Milne's *The Boy Comes Home* which was a great success. He also took on the role of Advisory Editor of *News & Views*, a student newspaper which he helped establish. In 1940, Davis took over the coaching of the First XVIII from Billy Morcom but it was for just one season. On 6th July, the boarders presented him with a handsome entrée dish as a token of what he meant to them in the years he was with them. He had resigned as a resident master as he was about to marry Caulfield's kindergarten teacher Joan Johnson.

When I was writing Stan Kurrle's biography, I asked him about his teachers. He rated Bob Horne, who taught English, and Harold Pennefather, his history master, very highly but reserved his highest praise for the chemistry teaching of Davis Hughes.

To support the war effort, Davis conducted night classes at Caulfield in mathematics for navigation for those awaiting call-up for the RAAF. He took leave from Caulfield in 1941 and joined the RAAF as an instructor in navigation, initially at Somers in Victoria then at Parkes in New South Wales, eventually becoming Squadron Leader Hughes.

At war's end, Davis returned to Caulfield where the December 1945 issue of the school magazine recorded that "Next year Squadron Leader Davis Hughes BSc is due to resume his work in the senior school after four years in the RAAF". He returned to most of the duties he had undertaken before the war but it was not to be a long stay.

In 1947, Davis accepted a position at The Armidale School in New South Wales where, again, he was recognized as a capable and popular teacher. He became Housemaster of Tyrrell House and involved himself in the school's theatrical productions. A great deal of work was put into an open-air play *Will of Stratford* which was to be performed at the end of 1947. An amphitheatre was built by the boys but, owing to rain, the performance was hurriedly moved indoors. In 1948, Davis produced *Tobias and the Angel* by James Bridie.

At various times during his stay at Armidale, Davis was master-in-charge of boxing, gymnastics and cricket and, in 1949, was appointed Senior Assistant Master, effectively Deputy Headmaster.

Early in first term 1950, Davis was elected to the New South Wales Parliament as a Country Party member at a by-election and was re-elected at the general election in June. He was voted leader of the party in 1958.

And then came the bombshell in 1959. His BSc, claimed since the 1930s, was a degree of his own creation. Was it the end of his career? Far from it! Although he lost the leadership, he was returned to parliament at the next election with an increased majority and he held the seat of Armidale for 22 years 11 months and seven days until his retirement in 1973.

In May 1965, the Labour government of Jack Renshaw lost the election and the Liberal/Country coalition came into office under Robin Askin. Davis was appointed Minister of Public Works with the responsibility for tackling the cost blow-out of the Opera House project. There began what was to become a most difficult relationship between Davis and the Danish architect of the Opera House, Jørn Utzon.

Davis sacked the Opera House Executive Committee and decided to run the whole show himself. By the end of the year, the relationship between architect and minister had soured substantially. Davis refused to accept Utzon's approach to management, to the building of plywood prototypes for the interior and the high costs of proposed stage machinery. Utzon wanted to be in control of every detail. Davis tightened the screws. Utzon could tolerate it no longer and left the job in March 1966.

Another architect was engaged and the Opera House was not finished to Utzon's design. It was a cost-saving compromise which omitted many of the internal elements which would have made it a real opera house. Steps are now being taken, nearly 50 years after it was officially opened, to retro-fit the necessary components to make an opera house out of the concert hall it became.

Davis left parliament in 1973 and was appointed Agent-General for New South Wales in London where he remained for five years. In 1975, he was knighted and made a Freeman of the City of London. In 1996, he received the honorary degree of Doctor of Education from the University of Newcastle for his role in de-centralising the state education system and the provision of state aid for non-government schools.

He made his only return visit to Caulfield in 1994. He joined Principal Stephen Newton and me for morning tea, marvelling over the changes to the school in the 47 years since he had left.

Davis died on 16th March 2003. Although Utzon had no

contact with Davis for 30 years, he sent a moving message of condolence to Lady Hughes. He was ever a gentleman.

Agnes Milowka

1981 – 2011

Agnes was not one of the first girls to come to Caulfield Campus but she was certainly a pioneer in many ways.

Born Agnieska Milówka in Częstochowa, Poland, on 23rd December 1981, she came with her family to Melbourne at an early age. She arrived at Caulfield in 1994 on an academic scholarship which was repaid in so many ways.

Over the following six years, Agnes was involved in practically every activity that was open to her. In her very first year, she joined the cross-country squad and remained a member throughout her time at Caulfield. She also took up rowing and was a member of the First VIII from 1997 to 1999. In her final year, she was Captain of Boats which involved her in leadership of a three-day training camp at Geelong and another of nine days' duration in Canberra, coming second to a university crew in a regatta on Lake Burley Griffin.

Given that Agnes arrived on an academic scholarship, it was no surprise that she won an absolute catalogue of academic prizes in each year through to Year 12 and received School Colours for Academic Excellence – and, of course, for rowing.

She was not, however, merely a clever girl who could row.

Agnes also involved herself in the cultural life of the school. She danced in the 1996 production of *Fire and Rain*, written and directed by Joachim Matschoss and demonstrated her practical skills by working on set construction and on the backstage crews of *Cosi*, *The Brick and the Rose* and *Noises Off*.

In 1998, Agnes was vice-captain of Davies House, a leader on a Year 8 camp at Yarra Junction, a peer support leader, Open Day guide, and took part in the Amnesty International Candle Day.

Her Year 12 was just as busy as she became Co-Captain of Davies House and a member of the School Committee, editor of *Extempore* and assistant editor of *The Caulfield Grammarian*.

At the end of 1999, Agnes told me that she had no idea what she would go on to do but I knew full well that whatever she did she would do it well and do it with a smile.

Like many of Caulfield's brightest, Agnes went on to the University of Melbourne where she graduated with a Bachelor of Arts degree in History and Australian Studies. Perhaps being a schoolgirl rower was enough of an on-water activity for her. At Melbourne, she joined the Underwater Club and, naturally, became president in 2005. Then it was on to Flinders University to study maritime archaeology. As with everything she did, she wanted to do more so she completed an internship in St Augustine, Florida, where she participated in the archaeological excavation of historic shipwreck sites.

Before she returned to Australia, she was introduced to the extensive cave systems in Florida which she began to explore as well as researching and diving in a series of archaeological projects.

Back in Victoria in 2009, Agnes and another diver explored the Elk River streamway cave system by an additional 4,600 feet. She also dived at Cocklebiddy on the Nullabor Plain in 2009, which was recorded as the longest cave dive in Australia by a female. She had reached the mid-point of a dive by Craig Challen who became famous in 2018 for his part in rescuing the Thai soccer team and their coach.

With her underwater camera, Agnes travelled to the Bahamas at the end of 2009 where she joined a National Geographic Magazine team as a photographic assistant.

Continuing her cave diving in 2010 in Florida, she laid over 13,000 feet of line across several cave systems, even making a connexion between two cave systems, adding 10,000 feet more passage. She also became a television personality, editing and presenting *The Agnes Milowka Project* featuring underwater cave footage. She also published over 20 articles about underwater exploration and her work as a diver.

Could Agnes do anything else? Well, yes! She acted as a stunt double for two female characters in James Cameron's film *Sanctum* and worked as dive instructor to the actors.

Continuing alone to explore a tight restriction in the Tank Cave near Tantanoola in South Australia, it all went wrong. Agnes ran out of air and died. She knew it was a risky business but she was an expert and accepted the risks, always maintaining her lovely smile.

A number of awards have been named in her honour as have several underwater geological features. Her smile would broaden even further to learn that in the sci-fi webcomic *Crimson Dark* the alliance starship has been named the A.W.S. Milowka.

Bill Morgan-Payler

1946 – 2006

Although he had been at Caulfield since 1958, my first close encounter with Bill was in 1963 when we debated against each other in the inter-house competition and then together as members of the school's A Grade inter-school team.

Bill was born on 23rd May 1946 and grew up on Phillip Island where his parents were farmers. His grandfather, an Anglican Archdeacon, had come to Australia where it was believed the climate would aid his recovery from tuberculosis.

Bill started his education at Cowes Primary School and came on to Caulfield as a boarder in 1958, maintaining a fairly low profile. His housemaster, Martin Carlson, remembers him sticking close to the other boys from Phillip Island, a place he was proud to be from.

By 1960, he had joined the Scout troop and tried his hand at rowing, starting in the Beginners IV which won its section in a couple of regattas. The following year, he rowed in the Fifth VIII, coached by the legendary Harold Pennefather who had introduced rowing to Caulfield a few years earlier and after whom the school's rowing club is named.

Bill easily accounted for nine Intermediate subjects in 1961 and five Leaving subjects in 1962. Rowing in the Third VIII that year, he began to experience injuries which prevented him from continuing further with sport. As a debater, he prepared carefully and took the business of debates very seriously.

Despite Bill's left-wing and anti-religious views, Martin Carlson had no hesitation in appointing him a House Prefect in his final year. Martin saw Bill as energetic and enthusiastic and there was nothing about him which failed to strike a favourable chord. A solid Matriculation pass in 1963 saw him off to university where he was one of the first intake at the new Monash University Law School.

I followed Bill to Monash the next year and it was a very interesting place in those days. Most of the students and staff quickly learnt who was who in the relatively small student body. Tall and rather well-presented, Bill fitted easily into the Law School but he had another side. He was an agnostic and his political disposition had become more radical than it was at school. He found an outlet for that as a member of the Labour Club.

After graduating, he taught taxation at the Prahran Institute of Technology in 1970 and completed his articles in 1971. He signed the Bar Roll in 1974 but resigned in 1977 to work as a solicitor for the Aboriginal Legal Service, first in Darwin and later in Victoria, reflecting his lifelong concern for the underprivileged. He was considered to be an outstanding advocate, perhaps illustrated in the case of *R v Bird Bill* in which our Bill convinced Justice Nader to fully suspend the sentence of a young aboriginal man who had embezzled over $500,000. Sadly for both Bills, the Court of Criminal Appeal did not agree. Bill returned to the Victorian Bar in 1981.

For a little over a decade, he practised mainly as a defence counsel so it was a change of direction when he was appointed to the Office of the Director of Public Prosecutions in 1994. Such were his forensic skills, courtroom manner and complete fairness that he was appropriately appointed Chief Crown Prosecutor.

Amongst a file of significant cases, Bill prosecuted Greg Domaszewicz for the murder of Jaidyn Leskie in 1997 and in the High Court for the respondent in the sexual offences case of *Palmer v The Queen* in 1998. Closer to home, it was Bill who successfully prosecuted Caulfield Grammarian Matthew Wales for the murder of his mother and stepfather in 2002.

In 2004, Bill was appointed a judge of the County Court of Victoria but his term of office was to be cut short by ill health. Even after he was diagnosed with cancer, Bill continued his court work as long as he could.

The Chief Judge of the County Court, Michael Rozenes,

wrote in his obituary for Bill that he "brought to this Court the very broadest knowledge of criminal law and procedure, together with a unique experience in the conduct of difficult criminal trials and appeals". Bill was also known for his sense of humour but it sometimes got the better of him. Early in his career, he was appearing for a defendant charged with offensive behaviour arising out of public masturbation. Bill informed the magistrate that his client had changed his ways and now had his problem firmly in hand!

Aside from his wife, Tina, and their two sons, Bill's other love was fishing. He was President of the Fly Fishing Association of Victoria and frequently made trips to Tasmania with friends to spend time with rod and reel. He continued fishing until he was physically unable to do so. Bill died on 10th June 2006.

Stuart Pink

1968 – 1995

When I first met Stuart Pink, it looked as if he had everything going for him. Soon after he arrived at Caulfield in 1981, he involved himself in track and field athletics, tending to concentrate on distance events for which he had the right physique. He took his athletics seriously, trained hard and competed regularly. He was always among the first to book a place on interstate training camps.

The squad trained at school, at Olympic Park and, in 1983,

Stuart joined the residential camp at Caulfield Campus which involved sessions at Olympic Park, runs to Caulfield racecourse and up the Maroondah Dam. The following year, the squad ventured further afield to Canberra and the National Institute of Sport, visiting the Royal Mint and the National War Memorial.

During the August-September holidays in 1982, Stuart went on one of the more unusual excursions Caulfield conducted – to an uninhabited island in the Whitsunday Passage. The party consisted of 41 boys from Years 7, 8, 9 and 10, led by staff members George Mitchell and David Penman and George's wife, Mary. The group flew to Queensland but returned by coach via Carnarvon Gorge, Lightning Ridge and Parkes. The sheer fun they had leaps from every sentence Stuart wrote for *The Caulfield Grammarian* at the end of the trip.

Although he was not strictly a member of the swimming team, Stuart joined the swimming camp in January 1984. Coaches John Raven and Howard Tarpey drove the group to Ulladulla and Narooma where training and competition filled the days. From Stuart's article for the school magazine, it is clear that the camp was a great success.

Sometime in 1985, things started to change for Stuart. The normally quiet boy I knew through athletics allowed his school work to slide and some people who taught him said he became difficult to manage in class. It was to be his last year at Caulfield and I lost contact with him.

Stuart was born on 2nd December 1968 and was adopted soon

afterwards by Jan and Lance Pink. He grew up in a strict but loving family in the affluent suburb of Mount Waverley and attended the local primary school. Neighbours remember him as a generally quiet and friendly boy who pounded the pavement training for athletics.

In an interview with Michelle Pountney of the *Herald Sun* in March 1996, Stuart's parents said they believed his involvement with drugs began when he was about 13 and experimenting with marijuana. In hindsight, his occasional absences from class and leaving the school grounds, for which he was punished, may have been for a more sinister purpose than was thought at the time.

In the decade after he left Caulfield, Stuart's life spiralled downhill. He was in and out of work and in strife with the law, serving at least one spell of periodic detention. It was all brought home to one of Stuart's classmates, Brian Sidlo, after a chance encounter in St Kilda in early March 1995. Brian recently reflected on that meeting:

> *It was in 1995 and I was living in a flat on Park Street, St Kilda. One morning, I was walking along nearby Fitzroy Street, passing a couple of guys, when one of them called my name. I stopped and looked at him. He was lean, with tight jeans and a mullet. He had a pair of metal crutches. I was pretty sure I didn't know him. How did he know my name?*
>
> *"I'm Stuart Pink," he said. "Don't you remember me?"*
>
> *Wow. Stuart Pink.*
>
> *Yes, I remembered him. We'd gone to high school together.*

He'd left school early, before Year 12. I hadn't known him particularly well but for the first few years he seemed a regular kid. As he got older, he started going off the rails, picking fights and causing trouble. He looked a lot older now, older and harder. Which shouldn't have been surprising – the last news about him was that, a few years out of school, he'd gotten into heroin and ended up in prison for armed robbery.

Now here he was on Fitzroy Street, staring at me intently. Not in a menacing way, though. It was as if he <u>needed</u> me to remember him.

I apologised - of course I remember you, I told him. I felt flustered. We made some small talk, while his mate looked on. I motioned to his crutches.

"So, err, you stuffed up your leg, huh?" I asked.

He paused, sighed and looked at me. "Brian, I've stuffed up my <u>life</u>."

I wasn't sure what to say. "Umm . . . what do you mean?"

He looked at me sceptically. "Didn't you hear what happened to me?"

"I . . . ah . . . heard you robbed a milk bar."

He nodded. "Yeah," he said, regretfully. "Milk bars, 7-Elevens, TABs." He looked away, and shook his head. "I just don't know what I was doing."

We stood there for a few seconds, until I asked him, awkwardly, "So . . . what are you up to now then?"

Just as I said that, his mate told him they needed to get going.

As Stuart started to leave, he looked at me and said, "To be honest, right now I'm just waiting to die."

He held my eye for a couple of seconds, then turned and walked down Fitzroy Street on his metal crutches.

What did he mean by that? Talking to old school friends about the encounter, we wondered if maybe he had AIDS. In 1995, that was pretty much a death sentence. Or perhaps he was just despondent and had given up hope.

Stuart's story came to a tragic end just a few days later on Saturday, 11th March. In his 6th April 1997 article in the *Sunday Age*, John Silvester described what happened: "Pink was walking down Park Street, St Kilda, unaware that behind him were two paid killers, one in a car and the other on foot. The hitman on foot stepped up to Pink and fired three shots from a .22 pistol". Stuart was shot twice in the head and once in the shoulder. He died a few hours later in hospital. When he told Brian Sidlo that he was waiting to die, it seems he was speaking literally. He was a marked man, remorseful for his past but unable to stop making bad decisions.

Two days after Stuart's death, a very sad death notice appeared in the *Herald Sun*. It had been placed by Stuart's girlfriend. They had a baby son and were due to be married in July. That little boy would now be the same age that Stuart was when he lost his life.

When Mende Georgiev was put on trial for Stuart's murder, Stuart was described as a standover man and street-level heroin dealer. Silvester told his readers that Stuart could make a lot of money but the police stated that he was a young man whose ambitions exceeded his abilities. He had begun to fail to meet his financial obligations to his suppliers. Despite warnings, he started ripping off fellow drug dealers and this could not be tolerated.

The evidence adduced by the Crown in the case against Georgiev was that Stuart would either approach heroin users and offer to sell them heroin and then only give them a substitute, pocketing the money he gained to purchase heroin for himself; or he simply robbed other drug dealers, acting alone or sometimes with another man. Stuart would use a pocket knife to threaten his victims, stealing cash, jewellery and drugs. During one of these robberies, committed only a few days before his death, Stuart stabbed drug dealer Tomislav Juricic who was a friend of Georgiev. Stuart's murder was "pay back". The killing took no more than 30 seconds.

Georgiev was found guilty and sentenced to 20 years' imprisonment with a non-parole period of 16 years.

My only memories of Stuart are those of a hard-working and friendly young athlete who enjoyed his sport and had great fun on various camps, about which he wrote accurate and well-crafted reports for the school magazine. I was much saddened to learn of his later life and particularly the manner of his death.

Ralph Skitch

1919 – 2005

Ralph Skitch was born in Wilcannia in New South Wales on 8th February 1919. His mother did not like the outback life so, soon after Ralph was born, they moved to Adelaide.

There were two more children and they grew up in a politically active family. Ralph's father was a member of the Labour Party and was three times unsuccessfully endorsed for Federal seats in South Australia. His mother was, in 1958, the first woman endorsed as a Labour Party candidate in South Australia. At the end of polling day, she had led on the primary vote but was only beaten in the seat of Thebarton after the distribution of preferences. Often thought of as communists, the Skitches could not have contrasted more starkly with the generally conservative families of their neighbourhood in 1920s and 30s Adelaide. After completing his secondary education, he qualified for a Trained Primary Teachers Certificate but his teaching career was to be briefly put on hold.

By 1939, the Second World War had started and Ralph was 20 years old. He was a conscientious objector. As such, he could be conscripted for service in the armed forces but only for non-combat duties within Australia. On 8th January 1940, Ralph attended the Unley Drill Hall, knowing he was to be required to swear the conventional oath of allegiance. He refused to do so.

On 9th September 1940, Ralph was prosecuted in the Adelaide

Magistrates' Court under Section 76 of the *Defence Act*.

Ralph's lawyer submitted that the form of the oath he had been asked to swear was wide enough to require him to serve outside Australia and that the words "within the Commonwealth" should have been inserted in the form. Ralph wanted the wording of the oath to be adjusted so it would not refer to possible overseas service.

After a two-day hearing in which Ralph protested that he was not a communist, the magistrate found that he was and that he had refused to take the oath because of his political beliefs. He sentenced Ralph to six weeks in gaol.

Ralph appealed to the High Court of Australia, sitting in Melbourne, which heard the case of *Skitch v Pratt* on 24th October. Pratt was the army captain who had attempted to administer the oath on 8th January.

One of the three judges, Mr Justice McTiernan, expressed "doubt as to whether the form of the oath tendered was appropriate to the appellant's case" but the court upheld the magistrate's decision although it removed the prison sentence. Ralph was ordered to pay costs of £10 and a fine of £1. The case received wide press coverage.

To escape public reaction to the publicity, Ralph moved to Brisbane and, in 1943, to Rockhampton where he taught at Rockhampton Boys' Grammar School and also coached cricket, even donating a trophy for prowess in the sport.

In 1945, Ralph began his long association with Malvern

Memorial Grammar School and Caulfield Grammar School. He had married Elsa Berglind in Queensland in early 1944 and a daughter was born later in the year, prior to their move to Melbourne where they settled in Mount Waverley.

Reading through issues of *The Malvern Grammarian*, one comes across cricket report after cricket report praising Ralph's coaching and his ability to teach young players the finer points of the game. Soon he was coaching the School XI and the captains' reports echo those I have mentioned.

There was, however, another side to Ralph. In Andrew Joseph's book, *My Malvern Grammar*, he describes Ralph as "terrifyingly strict" and "erratic and angry" and that "he could be caustic, sarcastic and constantly abrasive". He does give Ralph credit for his "serious wish, indeed, his insistence, that he impart knowledge to his students". He also points out that Ralph "seemed able to project a relaxed and balanced good humour in social situations that was frequently lacking in the classroom".

With the amalgamation of Malvern and Caulfield in 1961, Ralph was one of the small group of secondary teachers to come to Glen Eira Road.

In his first year at Caulfield, Ralph taught mathematics and coached Under 14B cricket and Under 14A football. He played in the Staff v Boys football match in 1962. The staff team was described in The Caulfield Grammarian as "inept but sincere" – and the boys won easily.

From 1963 until he left Caulfield in 1969, Ralph coached

the Second XI and sometimes the Third XI, known as the "Gentlemen's XI". Whether it was cricket or football, the reports are the same: "Mr Skitch must be thanked heartily for the time and interest he put into the team and it was through his coaching that the season became very enjoyable". So said the captain of the Second XI in 1964.

I was not in any of his classes but, in 1963 and 1964, I was a member of the Second XI cricket squad. I was a wicket keeper and batsman of only moderate ability but Ralph painstakingly helped me to improve and that contributed to my lifelong love of the game.

Some of Andrew Joseph's criticisms of Ralph were echoed by colleagues at Caulfield. One went so far as to say that Ralph was totally unsuited to teaching, that he disliked young people and was prone to violence in the classroom.

In the staff common room, Ralph was quiet and when he spoke he did so ponderously, as if he were weighing the effect of every word. Most lunchtimes, he sat at a corner table playing cards with Alf Di Battista, who also came across from Malvern, and any two staff who could be cajoled into playing. In 1967, Ralph was elected Chairman of the Common Room Association, a role he carried out with efficiency.

On 16th May 1969, he submitted his resignation, to take effect from the end of Term 2.

In the mid-1950s, Ralph's marriage to Elsa Berglind had broken down and they were divorced in 1961, just after Ralph had started at Caulfield. In 1963, he married June Newland who survived him.

After leaving Caulfield, Ralph taught for a while at a Catholic school and then in distance education. He died on 21st March 2005 at Gumeralcha in South Australia. He was 86.

Fred Walker

1884 – 1935

If you went to Scotch, you'd reckon Cyril Callister did it. If you went to Caulfield, you'd <u>know</u> Fred Walker did it. To be fair, I guess we could agree they both did it. Did what? Invent Vegemite!

Fred was born in Hawthorn on 5th January 1884. After his father was killed in an industrial accident in 1890, Fred was awarded a scholarship to Caulfield Grammar School by Headmaster Walter Buntine who must have had an inkling of what young Fred might go on to do.

He left school in 1899 and joined the produce and export firm of J. Bartram and Sons where he learnt about canning and refrigeration which were emerging food technologies. A fast learner, he was able to set up his own import and export company, Fred Walker & Co. in Hong Kong at the age of 19.

By 1910, he had been back in Melbourne for two years and began canning a variety of foods, including Red Feather cheese, for Australian consumption and for export to Asia,

South Africa and New Zealand.

Although Fred had joined the Australian Garrison Artillery in 1908 and had become an officer, he did not join the AIF when war broke out because of the importance of his role in food production which included exporting food to England.

After the war, Fred began to manufacture Bonox, a beef extract product which is on the shelves in every Australian supermarket to this day. In 1918, his company set up in Sydney and, in the following year, in Adelaide and New Zealand. Despite this expansion, Fred suffered severe financial problems, reflecting difficulties experienced by manufacturers in many countries after the war.

A major reconstruction of the company kept it afloat and, in 1923, Fred took a long hard look at the English product Marmite. He employed Old Scotch Collegian chemist Cyril Callister to develop a yeast extract product to compete with Marmite. In 1924, a public competition was held to find a name for the new spread. The name Vegemite was selected by Fred's daughter, Sheilah, from the entries which were submitted.

All did not go well. Initially Vegemite did not sell well so Fred changed its name and called it Parwill, a rather unfortunate joking reference to Marmite: "Ma might" but "Pa will". Not surprisingly, he soon returned to calling it Vegemite. Sales took off when he embarked on a promotion which involved giving away a free jar of Vegemite with every other Fred Walker & Co. product purchased. As a result, sales boomed and the company's fortunes rapidly improved. This allowed Fred to commence canning fish pastes and meat in Tasmania and Dandenong.

In 1925, Cyril Callister's experimental work led to Fred manufacturing processed cheese in Melbourne in conjunction with James L. Kraft of Chicago. The Kraft Walker Cheese Company came into being in 1926 and, by 1930, Fred's earlier financial problems had disappeared.

Jobs in Fred's companies were keenly sought because he offered workers a social club, allowed morning tea breaks and provided first aid and canteen facilities. He wanted to make factory work less arduous and introduced scientifically designed work systems which increased productivity which, in turn, led to the payment of handsome bonuses.

In 1933 and 1934, Fred was president of Melbourne Rotary and he supported the Boy Scouts' Port Melbourne Settlement for underprivileged children. He also spent some time assisting with the Lord Somers Camp.

After Fred died of heart disease on 21st July 1935, Fred Walker & Co. was purchased by Kraft Foods. Vegemite, of course, is now a staple of breakfasts all over Australia. Its success was assured during the Second World War when, because of its high Vitamin B content, it was included in Australian soldiers' ration packs – and is now served in trendy cafes on multi-grain toast under a layer of smashed avocado.

Stanley Kurrle

1922 – 2016

Stanley Wynton Kurrle was born on 30th September 1922. His paternal grandparents were German winemakers who settled in the Sunbury district and established the Rosenthal vineyard. Later, they moved their growing operations north to the Murray but Stan's father chose to be independent of the rest of the family and moved to the city where he built up a successful confectionary business from scratch.

Stan was enrolled at Caulfield in 1927, starting at the early age of four. He was taught by Arthur Astley, Billy Morcom, Robert McCullough, Gemmell Lamb Smith and Frank Archer. All of those men, except for Arthur Astley, were still teaching at Caulfield when I arrived 24 years later! Those who taught Stan recall his diligence, enthusiasm and co-operation rather than academic brilliance but he did make his mark on the school.

In 1940, his final year at the school, Stan was in his second year as a prefect. He had special responsibility for the Christian activity group, the Crusader Union, and for debating. He was Captain of Buntine House and a platoon commander in the Cadet Unit. He played in the First XVIII and featured prominently in house cricket, football and athletics as well as inter-house and inter-school debating. His contributions to *The Caulfield Grammarian* centred on reports of Crusader Union activities and reports of visitors to the school who spoke on Christian themes. He was also involved in the publication of *News and Views*, a student newspaper which was a forerunner of *Demos* and *Figleaf*.

Stan matriculated in 1940 with passes in five subjects and went up to the University of Melbourne to read medicine. When the Japanese entered the war, Stan unsuccessfully applied to join the RAAF as aircrew. If he could not fly. He did not want the RAAF at all so he joined the 5th Battalion, Victorian Scottish Regiment, and trained as a medical orderly. His unit trained at Rye in Victoria and was *en route* to Burma when the ship was turned back to Western Australia after the fall of Singapore.

It was in Western Australia that an incident occurred which gives us an idea of Stan's personality. He was dining in uniform at a hotel with some friends when in walked Lieutenant-General Sir Horace Robertson and his guests. Robertson was an ambitious and aggressive soldier who had distinguished himself with the 10th Light Horse in the Great War. He spotted Stan and his friends and sent a message to them to leave as he was not prepared to eat in the same dining room as non-commissioned personnel. Stan, quite rightly, refused to budge and Robertson was obliged to give way. Even at 19, Stan was not a man to back down when he knew he was right.

Encouraged by an army chaplain, Stan decided to study for the ministry and, as a consequence, was discharged from the army to commence a Bachelor of Arts degree at Melbourne in 1944. He played football and squash for Trinity College and was Secretary of the Inter-Collegiate Delegates, the body which arranged inter-college sport in the university.

Whilst studying for the Diploma in Education in 1947, he undertook a teaching round at The King's School, Parramatta, where the Headmaster, Denys Hake, offered him a job. He had also been offered a place at Melbourne Grammar School but declined both offers as he wished to gain some teaching experience in the United Kingdom.

He had applied to read theology at Oxford and filled in the time prior to the course starting by teaching at Liverpool College. At Oxford, he worked hard and played hockey and cricket.

In 1951, he returned to Australia where he married Lorna Wallis of Bendigo, honeymooning in Europe before he was ordained in Liverpool in May 1953. The Reverend Stanley and Mrs Kurrle moved to Lancashire where Stan had been appointed one of the assistant clergy in the nine-square-mile industrial parish of Sutton St Helens. There were lots of boys in the area and many were on probation. Stan successfully set about involving them in cricket and soccer teams. He also helped out with the Lark Lane youth group in Liverpool. The Rector said that Stan was the only man who could control the boys – and he achieved it with firm kindness.

Meanwhile, back at Caulfield, an announcement was made which would have a profound effect on Stan's life. The headmaster, Frank Archer, had decided to retire and the School Council was seeking a replacement.

Frank Gaunson, a member of the School Council, raised the issue of Stan applying for the headship with Oscar Kurrle, Stan's father, who wrote to his son, passing on Gaunson's suggestion. Stan dismissed the matter as ridiculous. After all, he had only taught for one year.

A little later, Stan's former classmate, Peter Karmel, wrote to him suggesting he should apply. Stan's reply was dismissive but, unknown to Stan, his father had taken the extraordinary step of instructing his solicitor, Harold McCracken, to put in an application on Stan's behalf.

Other voices were telling Stan to apply so, on 28th July 1953, Stan sent a cable applying for the post. Formal applications were received from 21 applicants and the list was impressive, several going on to be headmasters elsewhere.

The first short list of five was reduced to three: Stan, W.H. Mason Cox of Wesley College, and Lindsay Thompson, then teaching at Melbourne Boys' High School.

In the middle of the afternoon on Friday, 18th September, the telephone rang at 126 New Street, St Helens, and Lorna Kurrle wrote down the text of a cable from Australia. Her husband was to become the fifth headmaster of Caulfield Grammar School. He was only 31 years old.

Following an old and tired headmaster, Kurrle came to Caulfield when a young, enthusiastic headmaster was exactly what was needed. He brought a vision for the school which developed the work of Archer and took Caulfield from the second level of independent schools into the top tier.

Stan retired old and under-qualified staff and employed professional educators like Bill Callander who improved the academic standard of the school. He had plans for the school's farm and country centre at Yarra Junction and, thereby, to improve its educational role.

If you stand in the Buntine Quadrangle or the north quadrangle, virtually everything you see, with the exception of the Cripps Centre which replaced Stan's Memorial Hall, was built or added to in his time: the swimming pool, the McCullough science block and, further afield, the boarders' dining room, the boatshed at Albert Park and substantial improvements at Yarra Junction.

The school was in very good financial shape and, within a year of Stan's arrival, there were waiting lists at most levels. He tackled discipline head-on, suspending two 13-year-old boarders for smoking and subsequent publicity in *The Argus* pushed enrolments up even further. There were now 790 boys enrolled of whom 95 were boarders.

Aside from buildings, Stan developed the modern house system which operates to this day in pastoral care as well as a system for organizing games and activities. It is a system which has been copied by many schools in Victoria and other parts of Australia.

In late 1956, Stan held a conference of teachers and parents of boys in Years 10, 11 and 12. He welcomed parents and, after a brief introduction by the Chief of Staff, parents were given the opportunity of conferring at length and in private with subject teachers and form teachers about the academic performance of their sons. This innovation was a direct product of Stan's visits to schools in the United Kingdom where the practice of parent-teacher interviews was already well established. It was soon followed in other schools.

In 1958, Stan brought Caulfield into the Associated Public Schools of Victoria, probably the single most important step in the school's development. By 1960, Caulfield was a big school with 900 boys and 116 in the boarding house. True to his view that Caulfield had a role to play in the wider world, Stan supported a visit at Easter 1960 by the cricket team from Pulteney Grammar School, Adelaide. This was the beginning of games and cultural tours to various cities and countries which continue today. Stan also established a Community Service Group, assisting the Brotherhood of St Laurence, the Lord Mayor's Camp and Kew Cottages.

Once a week, Stan took the Year 12s for a discussion on a wide range of social and moral issues in a lecture theatre which is now the Fairfax Studio, recently converted for dance teaching. He was "The Boss". He knew us and we knew him. He was very much <u>our</u> headmaster and he genuinely cared about each one of us. He knew every boy and his parents and, surprisingly, a lot about them. No opportunity was lost to speak to a boy in the playground or to a parent at a school function or in the street.

Stan drove his powerful American cars at high speed, perhaps with the knowledge that God was looking after him. He flew his own aeroplane and, one day, was flying over the school showing the site to a visitor from overseas when, to his horror, he saw a near riot going on below. The then Director of Music, Norman Kaye, had driven his Austin-Healey sports car into the grounds and was being mobbed by a horde of students. We all copped it when Stan landed and, no doubt, had pushed the speed limit from Moorabbin Airport.

In 1963, Stan successfully applied for the headship of The King's School, Parramatta. His final year at Caulfield was managed with the same calm leadership, inspiring teaching and very apparent hard work which had characterized the nine years which had preceded it.

Stan was 43 years of age when he became headmaster of King's in January 1965. At the time, the school was operating on two sites and was in the process of re-locating from the middle of Parramatta to a property of some 304 acres about two miles from Parramatta. It was Stan's task to lead the school through a process of consolidation at its new site. The school's Parramatta buildings were sold but the money needed for the school's re-creation far exceeded what was available and it fell to Stan to spearhead a series of fundraising appeals.

The growth of the school in the 18 years Stan was headmaster was dramatic. Buildings of all sorts were erected and playing fields were laid out. The old chapel was dismantled and take, stone by numbered stone, to the new school site where it was re-erected. It was not only buildings which received Stan's attention at King's. He ran the school in a liberal and open fashion, conserving its essential and traditional values (like the military-style uniform) but, at the same time, moving it into a greater awareness of the rich variety which can comprise school life.

Stan increased enrolments from 872 to 1120, saw the farm's output increase threefold, involved boys in the selection of monitors (prefects), gave great latitude to the editors of the student magazine and increased the proportion of leavers who went on to university. He introduced a faculty system which allowed the delegation of authority and encouraged subject teachers to develop their own teaching. It had always been Stan's concern to improve the standard of education at all levels of both of his schools and many of his innovations had that end as their primary focus.

In 1973, Stan advised the School Council to take control of Blue Mountains Grammar School which was in severe financial trouble and it, together with the overseeing of Tudor House, a preparatory school at Moss Vale, became part of the wider school for which Stan took responsibility.

Stan retired at the end of the 1982 school year at the age of 60. He had served for 18 years as headmaster of King's. In 1975, he had been installed as a Canon of St Andrew's Cathedral and Her Majesty The Queen appointed him an Officer of the Order of the British Empire in 1982.

In his retirement, Stan spent much time on his sheep property at Mathoura in New South Wales, where he played an active role in the running of the property. He retained an abiding interest in his schools, visiting both for significant events. Stan and Lorna returned to Caulfield in 1981 to commemorate Caulfield's centenary and again in 2014 for a special assembly to mark 50 years since he left as headmaster. The lunch which followed was a joyous catch-up with former colleagues and students.

Stan was an "educational personality" who not only carried out the job of headmaster but <u>was</u> a headmaster. It was not his qualifications or his experience but his nature which made him a success. His infectious personality drew others along with him and ensured that what had to be done was done. His loyalty to his governors, his love of "his boys" and his great enthusiasm carried him through two highly successful headmasterships.

In October 2015, he wrote congratulating Oscar Loughnan who would become co-captain of Caulfield in 2016 – Stan had appointed Oscar's grandfather, Ian Macmillan, to the staff at Caulfield in 1960. Such was the nature of the man.

Stan died on 20th January 2016 after a short illness. Packed memorial services were held at both Caulfield and King's. By any measure, Stan was a great Australian educator.

George Fairfax

1928 – 1996

George Fairfax was born in the Mallee at Nangiloc on 4th April 1928. When he was two years old, his parents walked off their Great War soldier settlement farm, unable to afford the irrigation required to run it. The move to Melbourne solved that problem.

Living at "The Astor" on Beaconsfield Parade, George initially attended Elwood Central School and then secured a scholarship to Caulfield where he commenced in 1942. He immediately demonstrated that he was a very capable student. For his "corporate activity" he chose to edit "D1 Times", a Year 9 class newspaper. Later in the year, he took up shot put and managed third place for School House in the Under 15 competition.

In Intermediate in 1943, he undertook the NCO course at Rowville during the Easter vacation and was promoted to corporal in the Cadet Unit, passing the course with distinction. At the end of the year, he secured very high marks in all eight subjects.

It may well have been the 1944 school play which set him on the road to a life in theatre. He appeared in *Seven Keys to Baldpate* as Cargan, the crooked mayor, and is said to have been very convincing. He passed all five subjects that year and was the mainstay of the School House debating team, for which he was awarded House Colours, the team coming first in the house competition. He was also appointed to the

School House Committee.

George had been appointed a School Officer for the Dramatic Society in 1944 and for debating in 1945. He played Charles Wykeham in *Charley's Aunt* and was promoted to Cadet Lieutenant in the Cadet Unit. At the start of Term 2, he was appointed a prefect. He had been vice-captain of School House since the start of the year. His Matriculation results secured him a place in the Faculties of Arts and Law at the University of Melbourne in 1946.

Over the next few years, theatre played a bigger and bigger role in George's life. He maintained links with Caulfield, joining the Caulfield Grammarian Players, appearing in *And the Music Stopped* in 1950 and *Comas* in 1951, which won great praise from the critics.

He had withdrawn from his university courses in 1948 and, by the mid-50s, was working full time in theatre. He appeared in *The Master Key* and *Sunday Costs Five Pesos* in 1953, the latter at the Frankston Drama Festival. He was also working in film and radio. In the same year, he appeared in the inaugural performance of the Union Theatre Repertory Company opposite Zoe Caldwell in Jean Anouilh's *Colombe*. He appeared in all 15 plays in that first season, performing one play while learning his lines for the next one.

In 1955, George travelled to London, under the auspices of the British Drama Council, where he completed a theatre course and was selected for a television production course with the BBC. He also travelled extensively in the provinces, directing *Dial M for Murder* and *The White Sheep of the Family*.

Returning to Melbourne in 1956, George took up a directing post at the Melbourne Little Theatre (later St Martin's Theatre) in South Yarra, under another Caulfield Grammarian, Peter Randall. George remained there for 12 years as both director and actor.

His passion for the plays of Jean Anouilh came to the surface again in 1960 when he directed *Traveller Without Luggage* in which I played a young boy alongside Edward Brayshaw, Michael Duffield, Pauline Charlston and Agnes Dobson, some of the best-known actors in Melbourne at that time. The set was designed by John Truscott who went on to win two Academy Awards for film design and who designed the interiors of the Arts Centre.

In 1965, George won the Melbourne Critics' Award for Best Actor in *Dylan*.

Simply listing appointments can be a little dull but doing so does give a picture of the range of work which George undertook. He was Chairman of the Producers and Directors' Guild of Australia from 1969 to 1971, a member of the Theatre Board of the Australia Council from 1973 to 1976, Chairman of the Council of the Australian Ballet School from 1974 to 1976, and CEO of the Victorian Arts Centre Building Committee from 1972 to 1978. He became General Manager of the Victorian Arts Centre Trust in 1980.

George returned to Caulfield in 1981 to open the H. G. Lamb

Smith Arts and Crafts Centre and, in 1992, spoke at the Headmaster's Forum on "Arts in Australian Society".

After nine years at the helm of the Arts Centre, George decided to retire in 1989. He had seen the Concert Hall open in 1982 and the main theatres building open in 1984. He, quite literally, saw the project rise from the mud of the Yarra River to present Melbourne with a theatre complex which has few equals anywhere in the world.

Just before he retired, George took leave of absence from the Arts Centre to direct a revival of the musical *Man of La Mancha* with Graeme Murphy and followed that by directing Stravinsky's *A Soldier's Tale* for Summer Music. In 1991, he directed Ron Elisha's play *Esterhaz* at The Playbox.

Recognition of George's outstanding work took many forms. He was awarded the Queen's Silver Jubilee Medal in 1977 and appointed a Member of the Order of Australia in 1984. The George Fairfax Studio at the Arts Centre was named in his honour and a splendidly lifelike portrait of George hangs in the foyer.

In 1996, the University of Melbourne planned to confer on George the honorary degree of Doctor of Laws but the public occasion was not to be. He was suffering from cancer and was unable to attend the ceremony. The award was presented privately just a few hours before he died on 7th September.

His funeral service was held at St Paul's Cathedral which was absolutely packed. It was a theatre occasion like no other. Actors, musicians, singers and politicians paid their own unique tributes. A trapeze artist from Circus Oz, of which George was a strong supporter, performed above the nave. Paul and Mary Jo Kelly sang the traditional song *The Parting Glass* and David Hobson sang *I have lost my Euridice,* backed by the State Orchestra of Victoria String Ensemble, and George's own voice filled the vast space of the Cathedral. The service ended with prayers read by Canon Albert McPherson, Chaplain for the Arts, and Bishop James Grant, Dean of Melbourne.

As we left the Cathedral, we saw for the first time the banner stretched across the wall of the Arts Centre. It read simply "THANK YOU GEORGE!"

On 7th April 1987, George's widow Vicki Fairfax and daughters Jessica and Kaarin visited Caulfield to name the George Fairfax Studio. The theatre group of past students has been named the Fairfax Players in George's honour.

The Victorian College of the Arts has created the George Fairfax Memorial Award and the Arts Centre Melbourne, Deakin University, Castlemaine Festival and Swan Hill's Fairfax Festival all honour the legacy of a wonderful Australian whose life was driven by a passionate belief in the importance of the arts and in making them accessible to everyone.

Samuel Billigheimer

1889 – 1983

A paragraph in the 1964 issue of *The Caulfield Grammarian* recorded the retirement of Dr Samuel Billigheimer after 18 (actually 23) years of teaching at Caulfield Grammar School. The writer praised him for his "gifts and accomplishments in letters and music . . . his great scholarship, his devotion to the teaching profession, his intellectual honesty and the sincere interest in the welfare of the boys who came into his care . . . his dignity with humility and his warm humanity based on love of God".

Samuel Billigheimer (or Doc as we referred to him) was born in Mannheim, Germany, in August 1889. His parents' home was cultured and deeply religious with music being a significant element. By the age of seven, Samuel played the piano well enough to accompany his father who played the violin and, by 16, he was accompanying soloists, choir and even an orchestra for an oratorio performed in his final year at secondary school.

He proceeded to Heidelberg University, founded in 1386, where he studied French, English and Philology and was admitted to the degree of Doctor of Philosophy in 1911. His doctoral thesis was on the religious philosophy of the French intellectual Sully Prudhomme.

In 1912, Samuel began teaching at a girls' secondary school in Mannheim and then undertook further study in Geneva and at Freiburg University.

From 1922 to 1933, he taught at the Lessing Realgymnasium in Mannheim where he specialised in German literature and philosophy. Rabbi Dr Raymond Apple, in his 2008 lecture to the Australian Jewish Historical Society, said that Samuel's teaching methods included "the use of speech choirs, with voices creating a symphony of speech, though he admitted that this method could be abused as a propaganda tool".

After being removed by the Nazis from his teaching post in 1933, he became principal of the Lehrhaus in Mannheim, where he was also a board member of the United Synagogue, president of the Jewish Religious Association and a member of the Jewish Country Synod.

Samuel was interned in 1939 in the infamous Dachau Camp for five weeks. His wife, Gertrud, together with some of her colleagues, won his release from Dachau on condition that he left Germany.

It cannot have been easy for Doc to settle in at Caulfield. He was a German teaching German in a Church of England school, many of whose old boys had lost their lives in the war – fighting Germans. But settle in he did and the contribution he made to the education of Caulfield Grammarians over the ensuing years was enormous.

Throughout the 1940s, Doc not only taught German but became involved in life at Caulfield at many levels. In 1942, his two sons, Claude and Ludwig, were enrolled, and Doc gave several piano recitals of Beethoven sonatas. The following year, he gave a recital of several Bach preludes and his own interpretation of Beethoven's *Apassionata* sonata. He also combined his piano technique with his fine singing voice in a recital of Schumann's songs.

Over the years, the Art Club and Music Club both vied for his involvement. In 1944, he gave a lecture on "Typical Forms of Architectural and Sculptural Monuments in Southern Italy", speaking about monuments in Pompeii and Naples from the 1st to the 17th Century.

The Music Club invited him to perform a sonata program in 1945 and, in 1946, he spoke to the Crusader Union on "Movements in Modern Judaism". In 1946, the largest group of students and staff in ages turned up for a one-man concert by Claude Billigheimer, playing works by Bach, Kreisler and Schubert, accompanied by his father. It must have been a joyous occasion for both father and son and the audience loved it.

In the years after the war, the Goethe Poetry Prize Competition steadily grew in size. Over 400 students from 23 schools participated in 1952 and Doc was delighted when Carl Davis, one of his Intermediate students, won first prize. The prize-giving for the 1953 competition was held in the Philosophy Theatre at the University of Melbourne. Of the 12 boys who won prizes or honourable mentions, eight were from Caulfield, prompting the Secretary's comment that it was "a remarkable effort on their part . . . and a reflection of the enthusiasm instilled into them by their teacher".

The pattern had been set and, in the years that followed,

Caulfield boys won prizes and honourable mentions on a regular basis.

In 1958, boys in the German classes marked the 50th anniversary of the death of the poet and cartoonist Wilhelm Busch by performing his popular song *Max and Moritz*. Boys in Years 9 to 11 recited the seven tricks alternately and Don Wirth's slides of Busch's cartoons were a splendid contribution.

My chance to participate came in 1959 when German classes celebrated the bi-centenary of the birth of Friedrich Schiller. The program was framed by poems set to music by Schubert and Beethoven and included extracts from *Don Carlos* and *Wilhelm Tell*. Also included was an interpretation of Schiller's *Hymn to Joy* presented by a speech choir and a singing choir, carefully drilled by the Director of Music, Norman Kaye. After all these years, whenever I hear that piece of music, I can still sing a verse or two in German.

In order to put the learning of the language into a contemporary context, Doc made sure that classes were well supplied with publications about life in Germany. These came from the Press Offices of the German Federal Government, from the Embassy in Canberra and the Consulate General in Melbourne.

In 1960, the tape recorder which belonged to the Theatre Guild was used for the first time to assist in training of contestants in the Goethe Poetry Prize Competition. It must have done the trick as I managed to pull off an honourable mention.

The following year, Doc arranged for students to attend a performance of Kleist's *Der Zebrochene Krug* (The Broken Jug) at the University of Melbourne. Students also commemorated the 150th anniversary of the birth of Franz Liszt and the 50th anniversary of the death of Gustav Mahler, both of whom had interpreted Goethe's poetry.

By 1962, students taking German had shrunk in number. There was a Leaving class of five students and only one boy taking Matriculation German. Some attended a lecture which Doc gave on *Goethe's Faust in German Music* at the Victorian Branch of the Australian Goethe Society.

All the time Doc had been at Caulfield, he developed teaching aids which were published by the University of Melbourne and he also sent many articles to Germany for publication there. He maintained close links with the Semitic Studies Department at the University and was a member of the Hebrew Standing Committee. He took senior classes for the United Jewish Education Board on Sunday mornings at Toorak and on Tuesday afternoons at North Caulfield Central School, becoming headmaster at both centres. He remained with the UJEB for a decade after leaving Caulfield.

In 1961, the German Government recognized his contributions to the improvement in relations between post World War Two Germany and other countries with the award of the Cross of the Order of Merit (First Class).

Doc continued to lecture at the University, for the Goethe Institute, the Existentialist Society, the Victorian

Conservatorium, the Australian National Society for the History of Religions, and various Jewish student bodies.

He was a man of great warmth. My enduring memories of him include going to his apartment in Westbury Street to rehearse for the Goethe Poetry Prize Competition where we were made very welcome. He also gave me an "unofficial" prize. It is a now much worn paperback *Deutsches Musikleben* inscribed "To D.S. Thomson for his sound understanding of theatre problems. Speech Night 1962". It is a well-illustrated book on concert hall and theatre development in Germany after the war. I treasure it, even if I am not entirely sure what he meant by the inscription.

Samuel Billigheimer died on 17th May 1983, just short of his 94th birthday. Those who were fortunate to have been taught by him were greatly enriched by the experience.

Hans Ebeling

1905 – 1980

In his book, *The Complete Who's Who of Test Cricketers*, Christopher Martin-Jenkins described Hans as a "right-arm fast-medium bowler, turning the ball usually from the off but sometimes from the leg, an occasionally useful batsman but an ordinary field". The faint praise continues with statistics from a State tour to New Zealand in 1924-25 and his only Test at the Oval in London in 1934.

Hans Irvine Ebeling was born in Avoca on 1st January 1905.

His grandfather had emigrated from Germany in 1855 in search of gold and eventually settled at Avoca. His family moved to Elsternwick where he attended Elsternwick State School. He enrolled at Caulfield at the age of 14 and immediately stood out as a bowler in the forms' competition, in one game taking 8 for 51, and taking 3 for 10 against All Saints' Grammar School.

In the following year, he played football in the First XVIII and was promoted to the First XI for the match against St Thomas's where he took 4 for 10. He managed 4 for 30 against Trinity Grammar, 7 for 25 against Haileybury and 5 for 34 against Trinity College at the University of Melbourne. Across the 1920 season, he bowled 47 overs and took 28 wickets for 116 runs at an average of 4.1. Not bad for a 16 year-old.

Hans was appointed a Prefect and Captain of Cricket in 1921. He headed both batting and bowling lists, taking 58 wickets for 306 and scoring 322 runs with 82 as his highest score.

He continued as a Prefect and Captain of Cricket in 1922 and took 53 wickets for 371 runs. The football report in *The Caulfield Grammarian* commends him for his contribution to the First XVIII saying "Ebeling whose judgement in getting position, marking and accurate kicking were invaluable". To round off the sporting calendar, he won the 880 yards event in the School Championships, came second in the long jump and second in the open mile. He received the rare distinction of being awarded School Colours for football, cricket and athletics. At the end of the school year, he joined the Melbourne Cricket Club, going straight into the First XI and beginning a 59 year association with the club.

In the year he joined Melbourne, he was also selected for Victoria, playing for the state for the next 15 seasons. He had joined the Vacuum Oil Company (now Mobil) on leaving school and work commitments restricted his availability throughout the 1920s but he was able to travel to New Zealand with the Victorian team in the 1924-25 season. He retired in 1929 but made a comeback in 1933-34 following a discussion with the Collingwood captain, Jack Ryder, who asked Hans if he could help out the Victorians in a match against the Marylebone Cricket Club. As he was about to start his holidays, Hans agreed. He took 2 for 56 and one for 44 and made 68 not out.

He must have enjoyed playing against Jardine's MCC side because he made himself available for the next season, playing well enough to be selected for the Australian team to tour England in 1934.

Shortly before his departure for England, Hans returned to Caulfield to speak at a school assembly at which he was wished well for the tour. In response, Hans advised those who aspired to become good cricketers to practise constantly and to work hard. At the conclusion, the School Cricket Captain presented Hans with a pair of sleeve links bearing the school badge.

Hans had joined the committee of the Caulfield Grammarians' Association in 1928. In July 1934, a smoke night was held to farewell him. He was presented with a handsome silver cigarette case. Sadly, these, along with the sleeve links presented at the school assembly, were stolen from a display cabinet at the school in the mid-1980s. Fortunately, his Australian blazer and his "baggy green" cap were left behind.

The tour of England was not what it could have been for Hans. He played in only the fifth Test at the Oval as a replacement for the South Australian bowler Thomas Wall who was not fit. Hans had played second fiddle to Wall for most of the tour. In the fifth Test, Hans took 3 for 89 and made two and 81. On the bright side, he enjoyed meeting King George V and Queen Mary at Windsor Castle.

On his return from England, he captained Victoria again, winning the Sheffield Shield in 1934-35 and 1936-37. Sportsmen at that time were not full-time employees of their particular organizations. Hans recognized that he could not continue to play first class cricket as well as advance in his chosen work. He retired from playing cricket early in the 1938-39 season.

Hans had enjoyed an outstanding career at the Melbourne Cricket Club as a player and had joined the committee in 1934. In one office or another, he remained on the MCC committee for the rest of his life.

When war broke out in 1939. Hans joined the Royal Australian Air Force as a supply officer and reached the rank of Squadron Leader. Discharged in 1946, he returned to Vacuum Oil where he became, for a time, District Manager in Ballarat. This allowed him to travel each day from Avoca where he was able to look after his family's sheep farming interests. Distance did not trouble him; he made sure that he attended every MCC committee or sub-committee meeting – such was his commitment.

Invesigating storerooms at the MCC, Hans found stacks of old photographs. These now line many of the offices and corridors of the club and form a collection of international significance. If it had not been for his detective work, many may have been lost when the grandstand was demolished. He was also responsible for the development of the MCC museum which reached such a standard that a collector of cricket memorabilia, living in England, donated his unique collection to the museum.

Hans was Vice-President of the MCC from 1954-55 to 1978-79. In 1959, he joined a very select group as an Honorary Life Member alongside the Dukes of Edinburgh and Gloucester and some of the greats of the game.

As 1977 approached, Hans worked tirelessly to arrange the Centenary Test which was played in the second week of March. It was a spectacular occasion with every living Australian who had played against England invited to attend as was every Englishman who played a Test in Australia. Hans organized a commemorative stamp to be produced by Australia Post, a number of receptions and three nights of Open House at the club. By any criterion, it was a roaring success with 235 former Test players, umpires and officials among the 248,000 who attended the game, not to mention the millions who followed it on radio and television. In a fairytale ending, Australia won by 45 runs, exactly the same result as the first Test 100 years earlier.

Later in the year, Hans was guest speaker at the Caulfield Grammarians' Association annual dinner and gave those in attendance a taste of what was involved in putting the Centenary Test match and celebrations together,

In 1978, Hans was appointed a Member of the Order of the British Empire for his service to cricket. He was the first Australian to become an Honorary Life Member of both the Melbourne and Marylebone Cricket Clubs and, when he was elected President of the MCC in 1979, he was the first international player to hold that office. Unfortunately, his health broke down and he died in his first year as President.

Hans died on 5th January 1980 and was buried following a service at St Paul's Cathedral conducted by the Dean of Melbourne, the Very Reverend Tom Thomas.

The MCC has created the Hans Ebeling Award in his honour. It recognizes those who have given outstanding service to the MCC's Sporting Sections. He is honoured at Avoca Cricket Club where the Hans Ebeling Cricket Wall includes historic photographs of cricket at Avoca, a portrait of Hans and an outline of his achievements.

At Caulfield, the cricket supporters' club has been named the Hans Ebeling Club and its members wear a very distinctive tie. On display in the Lindsay Thompson Centre at the school are his Australian blazer and cap from the 1934 Test tour.

Alan Robertson

1926 – 2012

On Remembrance Day 1982, Royal Australian Navy Commodore Alan "Rocker" Robertson returned to Caulfield Grammar School 42 years after leaving to join the navy.

In his address to the school assembly, Alan spoke of receiving "the very great love of learning from two form masters, Bert Apps and Stan Lowe, who were outstanding men in a very distinguished group; not least, of course, was the headmaster, Frank Archer.

John Alan Robertson was born in Footscray on 11th September 1926 and began his education at a local central school before coming to Caulfield in 1938 and joining Buntine House. At the end of 1939, he passed the entrance examination for the Royal Australian Naval College where he commenced at the beginning of 1940 where he learnt to play rugby, sharing second row duties with Rothesay Swan who went on to become a Rear Admiral.

Graduating from the RAN College in 1943 at the age of 17, Alan went to war. His first posting was to the United Kingdom where he joined his first ship, HMS *Cumberland*, in 1944. Shortly afterwards, he went to HMS *Paladin*. Both ships were based in Ceylon. A minesweeping course in India followed in 1945 and, when the course was completed, Alan returned to the United Kingdom, joining HMS *Vanquisher* at Sheerness, a town in Kent which began as a fort to protect the River Medway from naval invasion.

After courses in HMS *Excellent*, he joined *Shropshire* for 18 months. In 1947, Alan served in HMAS *Australia*, then *Swan* and later *Lithgow* as part of the 20th Minesweeping Flotilla which was formed to clear the minefields in the New Guinea and Solomon Islands area, Torres Strait and the Great Barrier Reef.

Another sea-going posting took place to HMAS *Arunta* which was followed by service ashore at the Flinders Naval Depot, training young officer cadets at the RAN College.

Alan returned to the United Kingdom in 1952 for a period on exchange to the Royal Navy, specialising in communications. Promoted to Lieutenant in 1953 and Lieutenant-Commander in 1955, he settled in HMAS *Melbourne* for her commissioning. Postings to other ships followed before he was appointed Officer-in-Charge of the Naval Communications Station in Darwin in 1959. While he was there, he was also Executive Officer of HMAS *Melville* and, in mid-1961, he was appointed Executive Officer of HMAS *Voyager*.

In 1963, it was back to England and the Royal Navy Staff Course at Greenwich. Promoted to Commander, he served again with the Royal Navy in Singapore as the only Australian member of the Joint Planning Staff of the Commander-in-Chief Far East from January 1964 to December 1965.

This was a dangerous time and place as Indonesia's President Sukarno believed that the 1963 creation of the Federation of Malaysia represented a British attempt to maintain colonial rule, disguised by the granting of independence to its former colonies in the area. Actual conflict began when Indonesia launched a series of raids across the Malaysian border in January 1963. By 1964, "volunteer" raids had given way to the involvement of regular Indonesian troops.

Initially, Australia avoided involvement in what was now referred to as "Confrontation" but it was agreed that Australian troops would be used for defence of the Malay Peninsula. Attacks continued and Australian personnel were used in clean-up operations against the invaders. In 1965, the Australian government allowed a battalion to be deployed in Borneo. The British government also employed more aggressive action.

Australia's troop deployment escalated throughout 1965. Negotiations between Indonesia and Malaysia continued and the conflict ended in August 1966. Because of the secrecy surrounding the operations, it is not widely known that 23 Australian troops were killed during Confrontation and eight wounded.

In retirement, Alan wrote a scathing commentary on the official history of Confrontation in which he criticises Dr Jeffrey Grey's almost total omission of the navy's involvement and that of the RAAF. He debunks Grey's claim that we "won" Confrontation and points out that "it was financially crippling for Britain and little or no cost to Indonesia . . . perhaps Sukarno had the last laugh. After all, Britain began withdrawing its military presence east of Suez in 1967. Confrontation had been the last straw".

Alan returned to HMAS *Melbourne* in 1966 as Executive Officer and, in 1967, he commanded HMAS *Duchess* where he remained until he became Director of Naval Communications in 1971. Postings to HMAS *Hobart* and *Stalwart* followed and, in 1975, he was appointed Director of Naval Officers Postings with the rank of Commodore.

As retirement approached, Alan and Commodore Vernon Parker founded the Australian Naval Institute and it was through the Institute's journal, *Headmark,* that Alan continued to demonstrate his innovative thinking. In 2001, he published a book, *Centre of the Ocean World – Australian Maritime Strategy* and continued to write for a variety of publications.

The Australian Naval Institute established the "Rocker" Robertson Essay Competition which links his name with bright young officers of the RAN. The winner usually travels to the United States Naval College at Annapolis in Maryland and many of the winners' essays are published in *Headmark* and are widely read and discussed.

But why was Alan called "Rocker"? I asked a number of former RAN officers but none could tell me; they had always known him by that nickname. Over the Easter weekend in 2019, I had two very enjoyable conversations with retired Rear Admiral Rothesay Cathcart Swan (what a great name!) who is now 93. He had known "Rocker" since RAN College days and told me that Alan had gained his nickname as a young officer because of his passion for rock and roll music which was evolving in the early 1950s. So now we know!

After a long and fulfilling career, "Rocker" Robertson died on 20th June 2012 after a struggle with Parkinson's disease. It was fitting that he was farewelled at a chapel in Coffs Harbour, close to the sea.

Norman Kaye

1927 – 2007

Towards the end of Norman's life when Alzheimer's disease was tightening its grip, he lost most of his faculties but, strangely, he retained the ability to play the organ. His partner, Elke Neidhardt, would take him to a local church where the minister allowed him to play to the empty church until he was exhausted – and he played well. All the music he knew just came flooding back.

Norman James Kaye was born on 17th January 1927 and was educated at Geelong Grammar School. He studied the organ under the renowned Dr A. E. Floyd and was his assistant organist at St Paul's Cathedral until Floyd's retirement in 1947. Norman studied in the United Kingdom in 1949 and, two years later, became a music teacher and organist at Scotch College, Melbourne. In 1956, Stan Kurrle appointed him Director of Music at Caulfield Grammar School.

Not only did Norman set about the task of constructing what was to become a superb school choir at Caulfield, he also soon revealed his interest in theatre by becoming involved in the team of staff members who created the musical

Bullumbimbi which had its world premiere in the Memorial Hall in 1958. It may well have been the first musical written with an Australian Rules football theme. An LP recording made of the production demonstrates just how good it was.

Year by year, music developed at Caulfield. Classes were exciting and membership of the choir became positively fashionable. More recordings were made which featured the choir and, sometimes, the whole school in fine voice. Weeks of practice went into the mass singing which took place at Speech Nights in the St Kilda Town Hall. I have never forgotten belting out the toreador song from *Carmen* and other suitably roof-lifting pieces at successive Speech Nights.

In mid-1959, Norman travelled to the United Kingdom to further his studies, returning late in 1960 having been admitted as an Associate of the Royal College of Organists and an Associate of the Royal College of Music.

Those who were at Caulfield during Norman's 20 years on the staff will remember a man of extraordinary energy hurrying from class to class and almost flying down Glen Eira Road in his Austin-Healey to get to rehearsals of a play or concert in some other place. In 1964, he added to his already substantial workload when Margaret Scott appointed him as a foundation staff member at the newly formed Australian Ballet School.

Balancing music teaching with acting, Norman played leading roles in many professional theatrical productions and was presented with the Erik Award for Best Actor as Henry II in Jean Anouilh's *Beckett* opposite Edward Brayshaw in the title role. In 1963, he directed and played the lead in the school play, Fritz Hochhulth's *The Public Prosecutor*, in which I played Fouquier Tinville. He was a tough director but we students had great fun working with him.

In 1967, Norman was awarded a scholarship by the French government to study the organ and conducting at the Conservatoire de Nice, winning the Premier Prix at the conclusion of his studies under the great French organist Pierre Cochereau.

Prior to his departure for France, Norman supervised the installation and official opening of what was to be named the Archer Memorial Organ, the great treasure of Caulfield Grammar School sadly lost in the Memorial Hall fire in 2000. The pipe organ, built by George Fincham for the Congregational Church in Malvern at the end of the 19th Century, was bought by the school when the church closed. It was an outstanding instrument and worthy of the skills of Norman Kaye and the many visiting organists who came to the school to play it.

Television had also discovered Norman Kaye the actor. While still working at Caulfield, he had appeared in *Hunter, Division 4, Homicide* and in the 1976 mini-series based on the life of John Wren, *Power Without Glory*.

Leaving Caulfield at the end of first term in 1977, Norman continued his acting career without neglecting music.

He gave radio and television recitals and was a frequent commentator on music programs. In 1979 and 1980, he was Dramaturge and Director-in-Residence at the University of Melbourne.

In the 1970s, Norman began a film career that was to become a major focus of his working life for the next 20 years. For friend and director Paul Cox, he appeared in *Illuminations* in 1976 and in 15 other films in the years that followed. In 2005, Cox produced a moving tribute to his friend in the short film *The Remarkable Mr Kaye*.

Norman was nominated for the Australian Film Institute's Best Actor award in 1982 for his role in *Lonely Hearts* and, the following year, received the award for *Man of Flowers*. According to one of his friends, he used the trophy as a doorstop!

Man of Flowers was Norman's last leading film role. He had appeared in 30 films and 17 television series and had written the music for a number of feature films. He also continued to give organ recitals and make recordings.

His other films included *Mad Dog Morgan, The Killing of Angel Street, Unfinished Business, Turtle Beach, Paws, Oscar and Lucinda* and *Moulin Rouge*.

Paul Cox wanted to give Norman a major role in his 2000 film, *Innocence,* but it soon became clear that something was wrong. Norman simply could not remember the lines. Tests revealed that he was suffering from Alzheimer's disease. He was very upset when he was unable to continue with the leading role. Cox gave him a smaller role and a part in his 2004 film, *Human Touch*, Norman coming out of hospital for a few days at a time to complete the filming.

Precision and versatility were the hallmarks of Norman's career, one in which he demonstrated an extraordinary range of talents. But he was not just a skilled musician and actor. He was compassionate, modest, witty, and a loyal friend.

Following his death on 29th May 2007, Caulfield invited Norman's partner of 35 years, opera director Elke Neidhardt, to officially open the Norman Kaye Room at Caulfield Campus, a room specifically equipped for choir practice. The official opening on 22nd November 2007 was followed by a screening of *The Remarkable Mr Kaye* which was attended by Dame Margaret Scott and others who had worked with Norman at Scotch College, Caulfield, the Australian Ballet School and in theatre, music, film and television.

Organist David Agg presented a tribute to Norman Kaye organ recital at Our Lady of Victories in Camberwell in November 2007, and Move Records released a CD of Norman's music, including choral items and Norman playing the Archer Memorial Organ.

Frank Archer

1886 – 1958

I have no conscious recollection of my first meeting with Frank Archer, which is not altogether surprising as I was only four years-old. My mother had taken me with her to my enrolment interview. My first year at Caulfield was 1951 and I came across from Shaw House in 1954 where I saw the headmaster at assemblies but had no real contact with him.

When Frank retired and moved out of the accommodation at the school, he and Lillie moved to Grey Street in South Caulfield about 200 yards from my parents' house. Over the next four years, we met many times in North Road and Frank was always on for a chat.

Francis Henry Joseph Archer was born on 18th March 1886 in Ballarat where his father was a hairdresser and his mother a music teacher. He began his education at Urquhart Street State School and then moved on to Grenville College on a scholarship. There he excelled academically and was regarded as one of the best schoolboy cricketers in Ballarat. He was Dux of Grenville in 1902, passing in Latin, algebra, geometry and French, but failing in Greek.

He was unsure of the direction in which he wanted the future to take him so he decided on a year of "thinking time" and returned to Grenville where he redeemed his Greek by gaining honours at the end of the year. He also won the Cornwall Prize for the boy who performed best in studies and sport.

The Archer family was struggling financially so it was not possible for Frank to go straight to university. He needed to work to supplement the family's income. Ballarat Grammar School offered him a teaching post but it did not bring him any closer to university study so, in 1907, he applied for a position at Caulfield Grammar School as sports master.

It is widely known that Billy Morcom led the school's football team to 18 successive premierships but it is not so widely known that it was the work of Frank Archer which began the march to football success. He also involved himself in coaching cricket and athletics and he played cricket at various times with the Elsternwick Cricket Club and with St Kilda. In 1911, he was selected to play for Ballarat against a touring South African side.

Now that he was based in Melbourne, he was able to enrol at the university where he graduated with a Bachelor of Arts degree in 1910 and Master of Arts in 1912. He also completed the Diploma in Education, making him a very well qualified teacher.

Throughout the Great War, Frank took on many positions of responsibility which certainly equipped him for senior appointments. Supported by many in significant educational positions, he applied for the headmastership of the recently founded Trinity Grammar School in Sydney. Frank was appointed from a field of distinguished teachers from Australia and overseas. He duly resigned from Caulfield and he and Lillie moved to Sydney. They had been married a little over a year.

The Archers and Trinity survived the influenza epidemic of 1918-19 and the school grew in numbers. Frank and Lillie were highly regarded by the Trinity council, staff and pupils as well as by people in other Sydney schools. By 1922, Trinity had doubled in size. All was going well but there was an event taking place in Victoria which Frank could not ignore.

His mother's health was beginning to fail so he felt he had no choice but to return to Ballarat. Co-incidentally, Caulfield's headmaster, Walter Buntine, was planning an overseas tour and was seeking someone to manage the school in his absence. Buntine held Archer in high regard and offered him the post. Frank was appointed headmaster under Buntine who actually owned the school. Frank did an excellent job in Buntine's absence and, even after Buntine's return, he shouldered much of the role he had been caretaking. Buntine was happy with the arrangement as it allowed him time for other and very important duties.

Frank greatly increased the share of responsibility available to boys both as prefects and as members of sporting teams and activities. A form captains' conference was established and the house system was reorganized to allow more opportunities for boys to gain experience in administration and leadership, although house activities remained largely sporting until Stan Kurrle's headmastership.

Frank encouraged hobby activities and, in 1926, a hobbies exhibition was held. Such exhibitions continued into the 1960s. He introduced the modern subject of economics into the curriculum and also musical appreciation. The Dramatic

Society flourished and he established a reference library.

Unfortunately, Frank's heavy work regime took its toll and, in 1928, he sought medical advice after almost collapsing at an assembly. He was diagnosed with tuberculosis, then much more serious than it is today. Frank was sent away to a sanatorium and was absent from Caulfield for a year but returned in good health to his previous role.

Walter Buntine chose to retire in 1932 and the ownership and control of the school passed to a council. Frank was confirmed as headmaster in his own right.

Moving from Ardoch, a house on Merriwoola Street, to what had been the Buntines' rooms in the boarding house, brought Frank and Lillie into much closer contact with the boarders. Apart from attending church and going for walks (in pairs, at least) there was little for the boarders to do on Sundays. Frank opened up what had been the Buntines' garage, equipped it with tools and gave the boys the chance to make or repair things. He also introduced Sunday games – but only of a quiet kind so as not to disturb the neighbours.

Sitting in the comfort of the Cripps Centre auditorium today, students would be surprised to learn that, until the late 1950s assemblies were held outdoors in the Buntine Quadrangle. The assembly was controlled from a small dais in front of what is now Room 3. On the dais were the prefect on duty and the Chief of Staff (deputy headmaster). To the right of the dais were the prefects, to the left the staff. In front were the boys. The school was called to order and the headmaster came to the dais.

During the Second World War, Frank used the assembly to keep boys informed about fathers and older brothers who were on active service. He shared the grief of their death, the uncertainty of their being declared "missing" or placed in prisoner-of-war camp. And the joy he felt for those who returned safely. This was meaningful. Old boys shared their news with him in dozens of letters and he shared it with the school.

By the mid-1940s, Frank was toying with the idea of a rural centre for the school. At Trinity, he had experienced the evacuation to the country of the school during the influenza epidemic. He discussed with friends how Caulfield might give boys an opportunity to spend some time living in a rural setting.

David Cuming, who owned land at Yarra Junction, offered the school a parcel of land alongside of which flowed the Little Yarra River. The offer was accepted and, after much work and clever acquisition of military buildings which were no longer needed, Cuming House was officially opened in 1947. Until the advent of Newton Hall in China, a week or so at YJ was often the highlight of many a boy's year. It was the first rural education centre established by an Australian suburban school.

To visit a class at Cuming House, Frank often travelled by train to Yarra Junction and then walked to the farm. He loved to take part in the daytime activities and helped in the planting of a pine forest. In the evenings, he would gather boys around him and would read to them. Such was his infectious enthusiasm, many boys would seek the books he had started with them and finish reading them for themselves.

In 1949, Frank opened Shaw House, the primary section of the school, in Mayfield Street, a five-minute stroll from the Glen Eira Road campus.

Lillie Archer was a fine pianist and often accompanied students in their music examinations. Staff members were preparing to put on a revue for their own entertainment so Lillie wrote the music for a set of lyrics written by staff member Horrie Webber. The song that emerged is what we know today as the School Song – now treated somewhat more seriously than at its original airing.

Frank made his only visit to Britain and Europe in 1951 but, after his return, his health again troubled him. Late in 1953, he advised the school council that he would retire at the end of 1954. Pensions in those days were not what they are today so Frank gladly accepted an offer from Canon Wilson, headmaster of Brighton Grammar School, to do some sessional teaching. In a letter to a former student, he wrote: "I resume my humble responsibilities as a Form Teacher tomorrow and quite look forward to the 'Chalk and Talk'. It is much less worrying than the telephone, the mail and the 'someone to see you, Sir' programme." By 1957, he decided it was time to retire altogether.

All his life, Frank was involved in church activities. He chaired a committee of the Victorian Council for Christian Education. He was a councillor of Ridley College from 1934 to 1956 and a warden of the vestry of St Mary's Church in Caulfield. In 1948, he became a lay canon of St Paul's Cathedral.

Frank died following a heart attack on 19th February 1958. Archer House was named in his honour and, in the school's centenary year, the Archer Memorial Lecture was instituted in conjunction with the Victorian Chapter of the Australian College of Educators. Reflecting his love of music, the splendid organ installed in the Memorial Hall was named the Archer Memorial Organ. On 7th August 1992, the Archer Chapter of the Caulfield Grammarians' Association held its inaugural luncheon.

Gemmell Lamb Smith

1889 – 1951

Hugh Gemmell Lamb Smith was an extraordinary man who devoted his entire adult life to the service of others. That statement will come as no surprise to those who knew him or were taught by him. I never met him but heard about him almost from the moment I first attended Caulfield Grammar School in 1951.

Gemmell was born in Cheltenham on 31st March 1889. His father, who was a Moorabbin Shire Councillor, had come to Australia from Scotland and his mother from the West Indies. He attended a local primary school and moved on to Scotch College in 1901 when he was twelve. His mother ensured that he grew up with an interest in art and especially in music.

On completing his secondary education at Scotch in 1905, Gemmell chose not to go up to university. He became a teacher at Wangaratta Grammar School and later at Tudor House, at Chatswood Preparatory School, and at a small school in Gippsland before coming to Caulfield in 1913 as a resident master.

He had been a staff member for less than two years when the Great War broke out. One of the first contributions he made to the war effort was to organize a concert to raise funds for the Red Cross. Shortly afterwards, he joined the Australian Army but not as a fighting soldier. He became a member of the 2nd Field Ambulance, intent on saving the wounded rather than killing the enemy. The unit had been raised at Broadmeadows and it was there that he received basic training.

At dawn on 25th April 1915, he landed at Gallipoli. The Australian War Memorial records that "during the day, the medical services were overwhelmed. The suffering of the wounded was pitiful; many men died on the beach, and it is estimated that hundreds more lay in the hills out of the reach of help. There were inadequate arrangements for the critically wounded who could not be taken back to ships until after all the troops and stores had been landed.

It was early evening before boats became available; many of the maimed and bleeding were sent off in filthy barges". Gemmell was in the thick of it.

Several times while he was on Gallipoli, he sought treatment for enteric fever and, in November 1915, he was hospitalized in Egypt and then invalided home to Australia in December. Four months later, he returned to duty, re-joining 2nd Field Ambulance in France in August 1916 where he served through the horrors of trench warfare.

On 22nd April 1917, while evacuating wounded from the battlefield, he was shot in the left leg. He was immediately hospitalized but, after a month, returned to duty although the wound was not fully healed. He had another bout in hospital but, again, went back to his unit and continued to serve with them until the end of the war in November 1918.

At war's end, the Australian government then had to work out what to do with the thousands of men who could not be quickly returned home. It was clear that it could take at least a year for transport to be available to repatriate them all. As a result, the AIF Education Scheme came into being. Recognizing that the army had an obligation to aid service personnel to return to civilian life, opportunities were created for education and training for those who could not simply return to their old jobs.

Having been a teacher, Gemmell became one of the scheme's instructors and he also took the opportunity to study at London's King's College. As part of his study, he examined the approach to teaching of Caldwell Cook who emphasised the importance of making learning an exciting, inspirational and imaginative exercise for all involved.

Following his time in London, he returned to France where he also undertook study at the Academie Français before travelling to Australia at the end of October 1919. He was discharged from the army on 20th February 1920. Although he had, at various times, been promoted to the temporary ranks of Lance-Corporal, Corporal and Sergeant, he reverted to his original rank of Private on discharge.

Headmaster Buntine welcomed him back to Caulfield soon after his discharge from the army. Although he was in a rather fragile state and greatly affected by his horrific wartime experiences as a member of the Field Ambulance, he took to his school duties with great gusto, approaching his teaching with the view that, beneath all the group organizations inherent in a school, the individual was still the vital unit.

Aware of the need to acquire formal qualifications, Gemmell completed a Bachelor of Arts degree and, later, a Diploma in Commerce, at the University of Melbourne, all while he was fulfilling his roles at Caulfield. He was later responsible for the introduction of Commerce as an examination subject.

On 17th May 1924, Gemmell married Dorothy Harris, a kindergarten teacher from Turramurra in New South Wales. Like her husband, she devoted her life to others. Above my desk is a certificate appointing my father a Life Governor of the Royal Children's Hospital in 1956. The second signature at the base of the certificate is that of Dorothy Lamb Smith who was then the Secretary of the hospital's board.

Gemmell established good contact with boys of all ages and showed genuine interest in whatever they were doing and this extended way beyond the classroom. He believed in the value of boys having hobbies and being recognized for their skills. A Radio Club was formed and it held a successful exhibition which gave rise to exhibitions by other groups and, eventually, an exhibition involving all of them. They came together on the Hobbies Day which became one of the school's great annual events, bringing recognition to the exhibitors as families and friends poured into the school. Gemmell may have been the motivating force behind the Hobbies Day but it was the boys who did all the work.

Boys sensed that Gemmell was a warm and compassionate man and those who were lost or troubled sought him out. Some travelled to his bush shack at Killara, particularly those who needed their faith in themselves re-established. It was his experience with boys at Killara which convinced him of the value of the school's property at Yarra Junction.

His colleague, Eric James, wrote of him: "Yet, I think all of us who were closely associated with him in school life remember him most vividly as a man of supreme kindness, who always had time for people. Time for little boys, shy new boys, boys in trouble. In our memories how vividly we see him, for instance, on the morning of Hobbies Day, with shirt sleeves rolled up, moving briskly from room to room, with jokes and exhortations bringing order out of the first chaotic stages of preparation. We see him out of school, surrounded by cheerful groups, of which he was the animated centre; giving a brief and pungent message to assembly, or chatting with youngsters at the Tuck Shop, or along the oval boundary rallying the representatives of Davies House; a familiar figure at the School Play, usually in the box office; present at every School function; solicitously caring for a boy with an injury, or strolling around with an Old Boy, sharing cheery reminiscences. A member of staff cherishes the memory of his appearance in a classroom, when he came in to see some worried small boys who had lost some money they were responsible for. He banished their worries with a kindly word and gave them each the money in full, omitting to explain how it had been provided. . . He was in the deepest and truest sense a Christian man. He hated evil, but he never hated people. In every boy, no matter how exasperating or unsatisfactory he was, he saw the possibility of perfection, and never gave up hope of seeing it fulfilled".

After the first Hobbies Day in 1925 which spawned the annual exhibitions, it was clear that the ever-growing clubs needed somewhere to operate, other than classrooms, corridors and the yard. Gemmell's attitude was: "We want it, so let's make it". A carpenter was employed to supervise the building but the boys did the work. A single storey building, appropriately named Lamb Smith House was erected where Rooms 1, 2 and 3 are today. After many years of service to the Hobbies Club, the building was dismantled and taken to Yarra Junction.

As an original ANZAC, Gemmell delivered the address of remembrance on Anzac Day. For many years, Arthur Astley, who had been on the staff since 1901, read the names of the fallen. When he retired in 1940, Gemmell took over that role and, as the years went by, read the names of boys he had taught and known well. Throughout the Second World War, he had corresponded with every Old Boy serving in the armed forces. He also had small medallions made, less than an inch in diameter, bearing on their face the school badge and, on the reverse, the words ON SERVICE. One was given to each old boy serving during the war.

Boys at Caulfield underwent some form of military training since the earliest years of the school's existence. It raised its own Cadet Unit as part of the Victorian Volunteer Cadet Corps in 1885. This unit continued to operate until it was disbanded in 1929. It was re-established in 1941 and Gemmell became its commanding officer, a post he held until the end of 1948.

In 1931, Gemmell was appointed Housemaster of Davies House and he held that position with distinction until 1951. Another project he worked on for many years was the Memorial Hall fund. His vision was for a fitting memorial to be created in the school grounds to honour all of those Grammarians who had died in the Boer War, the Great War and the Second World War. He worked tirelessly and saw the funds raised but, sadly, the Memorial Hall was not built until seven years after his death.

Gemmell was twice Acting Chief of Staff when, in 1947 and

1951, Billy Morcom became Acting Headmaster during Frank Archer's absence on leave. He served as Chaplain of the Caulfield Grammarians' Lodge from 1948 until 1951 and, although not an Old Boy, was elected President of the Caulfield Grammarians' Association in 1951.

It was on Remembrance Day 1951, as he was reading the names of the fallen, that Gemmell suffered a severe stroke. He died on 26th December and was cremated following a service at St James the Great Church in East St Kilda.

The Caulfield Grammarians' Association commissioned artist Noel Counihan, himself one of Gemmell's past students, to paint his portrait which now hangs in the foyer of the Cripps Centre, which grew from the ruins of the old Memorial Hall which Gemmell had worked so hard to have built.

Aside from his work at Caulfield, Gemmell had been, at various times, Chairman of the St Paul's Cathedral Branch of the Church of England Men's Society, Treasurer of St James the Great Church in East St Kilda, Treasurer of the Victorian Amateur Athletic Association's Inter-Club Sports Committee (and a field games judge), Treasurer of the Caulfield Branch of the All for Australia League and a member of the British Association for the Advancement of Science.

Harold Pennefather

1901 – 1972

Harold was something of an enigma. Those students who had not been taught or coached by him might have dismissed him as a quiet, rather oddly dressed chap and left it at that. Those who knew him had the benefit of the wit, learning and passion of a remarkable man.

He was born on 25th May 1901, the son of a sheep farmer from New South Wales whose wife was one of the Irving sisters who founded Lauriston girls' school in Malvern. Harold grew up in Elwood, attending the local primary school before coming to Caulfield in 1912 as an 11 year-old. He returned to New South Wales with his parents and six siblings in 1914 but had been identified as a cricketer "with promise" and one of the best players in the Under 13 football team.

He completed his secondary education in Bathurst and proceeded to the University of Sydney where he commenced a law degree but did not find the study of law satisfying so transferred to an arts course, majoring in English and history.

In 1929, Harold returned to Caulfield as a resident master, continuing his studies at the University of Melbourne where he graduated as a Master of Arts in 1931. Over the Christmas break the year before, he married Doris Smith and they went on to have two sons and three daughters.

Appointed to Davies House in 1932, Harold took responsibility for house sporting activities and played a significant role in the development of the school library, donating important literary works as well as volumes on British history which were not easily obtained elsewhere. Along with other staff, parents and students, Harold donated trees which were planted to soften the landscape of the school.

As a member of staff with a motor car (not many did), he proved helpful when the Pigeon Club needed to transport pens which had been borrowed from the Elsternwick Homing Club for birds to be shown in the annual Hobbies Exhibition.

In 1934, Harold introduced monthly library notices listing additions to the school library and recommended reading. He aided in the formation of the student Library Club and was a regular adjudicator for the Debating Club.

At the end of 1937, Harold and Doris travelled to India for a holiday and, at a subsequent Old Boys' gathering, he entertained those attending with tales of their travels. With a growing family and an interest in continuing to travel, Harold supplemented his income by frequent weekend trips to the country cutting firewood for a local wood merchant and, in the Christmas holidays, working as a mail sorter when casual staff were needed by the Post Office to cope with the massive increase in mail at that time of the year.

Throughout the 1940s, he coached cricket and football and consolidated the teaching of history, at various times teaching Australian history, British history and Roman history. He also taught senior English and imparted his love of Chaucer to generations of students – and he made no attempt to hide the "earthy" bits, much to his students' enjoyment.

Sadly, Doris's mental health had deteriorated and, by the early 1950s, she and Harold separated although they never divorced. It was then that Harold returned to live at the school. To add to his distress, Robin, his youngest daughter took her own life, unable to cope with her mother's condition and the separation of her parents. Harold submerged himself even more into his work at Caulfield. He became Housemaster of Davies House in 1953 and a Year 12 Form Master and spent a lot of his spare time, when he was not playing golf, researching the countries he would visit when he retired.

In 1957, the House Notes section of *The Caulfield Grammarian* records that "the appreciation of the House is extended to Mr Pennefather for his attendance at almost every House function. His interest is greatly welcomed by team members". His profile was raised even further in 1958 when he and Guy Philpott joined Vic Nash to launch Caulfield into rowing in preparation for the school to join the Associated Public Schools of Victoria. With the cooperation of the Albert Park Rowing Club, the coaches and students practised very hard and eventually found they could sit a boat in any kind of weather. A new boat was purchased in readiness for the school's first row in the Head of the River in 1959.

Oxford graduate Jim Stanhope joined the staff in 1959

and he and Harold convinced Headmaster Stan Kurrle to introduce rugby the next year. Harold, of course, was well versed in rugby as he had spent his teenage years north of the border where it was the major winter game. Once rugby was established as a school sport, it inevitably became a house sport. It was at house rugby that I first came into contact with Harold. He took initial training with all the houses as there were very few staff who knew the rudiments of the game. It was not a very happy meeting between Harold and me. I could not get the hang of receiving the ball and running with it; all I wanted to do was get rid of it as soon as possible. Harold was not impressed.

Ian Macmillan joined the staff in 1960. He had rowing experience and joined Harold in coaching the growing number of Caulfield fours and eights. A few years later, Ian said of Harold, "We couldn't have a better organizer. Mr Pennefather is the heart of our rowing". At the Head of the River, Harold would stay on the river bank with the boys and cook steak and chops for them rather than retreating to nearby hotels where other staff had their meals. When work on the boats was needed, particularly the unglamorous task of cleaning, Harold rolled up his sleeves and got stuck into it. In his early years, Harold had done a little rowing with the Sydney Rowing Club. He had obviously picked up some very good ideas as his Caulfield crews enjoyed success against schools with a 90-year start.

His sporting skills were so diverse that he coached cricket and rowing, Australian rules and rugby. One year, when rugby was in its infancy at Caulfield, he was so keen and impartial that, for two afternoons a week, he coached the rugby XV and, for another two afternoons, the Third XVIII. Third term was when he rested; he only acted as an athletics official but was planning the campaign for the next year's crew. In January, he organized pre-season training for those oarsmen returning to school in preparation for the Head of the River.

In 1964, I was a member of Harold's Roman history class. My love of history had been instilled in me by my parents and I took to history classes with great enthusiasm. Harold never mentioned the rugby and we got along very well. His classes were meticulously prepared and always engaging. I still have my copy of W. Warde Fowler's *Social Life at Rome in the Age of Cicero* and will never part with it. Harold's Matriculation results in English and history speak volumes for his ability to convey his love of learning to his students. His philosophy of teaching and life can best be summed up in a word of advice and encouragement he once gave to a young master: "I don't expect boys to respect me because I am an old white-haired fossil, or because I have a degree, or because I can frighten them by wearing a big black gown; if I don't show respect, I don't deserve it; you've got to earn it".

On 26th April 1968, Harold and his colleague Lester Seward were guests of honour at the Old Boys' Dinner which marked their forty years of service to the school. At the end of Term Two in 1969, Harold's colleagues asked him to plant a *magnolia grandiflora* tree in the school grounds. It stands half way between the two main gateways and no longer needs the solid red-gum stake which Harold belted very firmly into the earth. Some time later, a bronze plaque was placed under the tree which reads:

THIS TREE WAS PLANTED IN MEMORY OF

HAROLD PENNEFATHER

A MASTER AT THIS SCHOOL FOR

FORTY-ONE YEARS

TEACHER SCHOLAR SPORTSMAN FRIEND

Four months later, Harold retired and almost immediately set off on a lone odyssey. Two of his former colleagues, Brian Bullivant and Ian Macmillan, were at Spencer Street Station to see him off, Ian just making it as the train was pulling out of the station. Harold's aim was to see the world but not on any sort of packaged tour. For more than two years, he travelled by aeroplane, boat, slow train, bus and on foot, visiting all the places he had read about. In London, he met Headmaster Bruce Lumsden and former student Russell Jackson and told them of all that he planned to see in northern Europe, on the Trans-Siberian Railway and in South America before returning home. This was not to be. He had arrived in Oslo in Norway, left his hotel room on the morning of 5th July 1972, walked down the stairs to have breakfast when he had a massive heart attack and died. He was cremated in Norway and his ashes were buried at Springvale with his wife and daughter. A memorial service was held at St Mary's Church, Caulfield, on 13th July and was attended by a large number of Old Boys, colleagues and friends.

Aside from "Harold's tree" in the school garden, the rowing club was named The Pennefather Club in his honour. He would be pleased with that. In 1963, a Year 11 student, Ric Hawkins, drew a very large and splendid cartoon of Harold. The original is with his family and a copy, which used to hang in the library, is in the archives.

Geoff Wilkinson

1929 – 1990

For those interested in school sport, Jim Blake's weekly column in *The Herald* was essential reading. On 2nd December 1978, he devoted his entire column to "Mr Tennis", his opening paragraph pointing out that, "In 1942 Geoff Wilkinson was a 'new boy' at Caulfield Grammar and today, 36 years later, he is still at Caulfield". Nine years later, he was still 'in the team'.

Ronald Geoffrey Wilkinson was born in Melbourne on 12th November 1929 and grew up in Brighton where his father worked for the Commercial Bank of Australia. Geoff attended Gardenvale Primary School where one of the teachers forced him to switch from writing left-handed to right-handed which caused the stammer which afflicted him for the rest of his life.

In 1941, Geoff's father was appointed manager of the Commercial Bank at Murrayville, between Ouyen and the South Australian border. Geoff attended the local school but sat scholarship examinations for Caulfield, one of the Ballarat schools and The Geelong College. He was offered scholarship places at all three but his parents chose Caulfield because they both had relatives in Melbourne. The choice of Caulfield also suited Geoff's tennis aspirations as he had been coached by Arthur Rogers in Melbourne and, if he came to Melbourne, he could continue with him. Geoff also knew Caulfield boys Max Hawley and Kevin Horton as they had played in tournaments which Geoff had entered. He had played in the Elsternwick Tennis Club junior tournament in the September school holidays and became a member at Elsternwick when he started at Caulfield.

A senior residential scholarship brought Geoff to Caulfield in 1942 and he immediately joined the First IV tennis team and remained a member until he completed Matriculation in 1946, captaining the team from 1944. Caulfield held the Associated Grammar Schools of Victoria tennis premiership from 1943 to 1946. Such was the standard of the team that it lost only one match in five years, against Camberwell Grammar School in 1942.

As well as playing tennis, Geoff was a member of the school's athletics team from 1944 to 1946 and played football in the First XVIII in his last year at school.

Unquestionably, an excellent sportsman, Geoff was also a high achiever academically, regularly being dux of his form. He had joined the school orchestra in his second year, initially as a pianist but later playing the double bass. His final year as a schoolboy was an exceptionally busy one as he was appointed Captain of the School in addition to his other roles. The year ended for him in style as he passed the Matriculation examinations, gaining honours in British history and economics.

Geoff's tennis was not restricted to Caulfield. In 1945, he was the Victorian Schoolboys Champion, having previously been the Under 12, Under 14 and Under 16 Champion and winner of a number of junior tournaments. He was a member of Victoria's winning Linton Cup teams in 1946 and in 1948 when he captained the team.

Tennis and fun combined in 1946 when Geoff was a ball boy at the Davis Cup match against the USA at Kooyong. He had attended coaching clinics at Kooyong conducted by Harry Hopman at Kooyong during the 1940s.

As a member of Elsternwick Tennis Club from 1942, Geoff began playing in the Lawn Tennis Association of Victoria Pennant competition when it resumed after World War Two. He played in Elsternwick's A Grade team from 1949 to 1957 and was Club Champion in 1953 and 1955. He later played B Special Grade for Royal South Yarra and for Caulfield Grammarians in the Old Boys competition. Elsternwick Tennis Club moved to join Dendy Park Tennis Club and it was there that Geoff continued to play into the 1980s, finishing in the veterans' team.

Although Geoff finished his secondary education at Caulfield in 1946, he returned in 1947 as a student teacher, taking up a resident master's post in the boarding house.

At the same time, he began the two-year teacher training program at Mercer House. In his early teaching career, he taught mainly in the junior secondary area and assisted in the physical education program. From the late 1950s, he taught mainly English, history and Latin in Years 8 to 10 and, after completing a Bachelor of Arts degree, taught English and history at senior levels.

The 1957 issue of *The Caulfield Grammarian* recorded Geoff's marriage to Norma Morris which took place at St Mary's Church, Caulfield, on 16th May. Geoff's teaching colleagues, Bill Sayers, Jim Pettifer and Vic Nash, were members of the wedding party.

In 1959, Geoff took on the important pastoral role of Housemaster of Archer House but relinquished that post when Headmaster Stan Kurrle appointed him Sportsmaster in 1961, responsible directly to the Headmaster for the administration of sport across the school.

When the Associated Public Schools of Victoria expanded from six to eleven, it necessitated the formation of a new committee to oversee inter-school competitions. It came into being in 1963 and Geoff became Caulfield's delegate and remained in that position until 1987 and was an honorary delegate until his death in 1990. He chaired the committee from 1973 to 1974.

As his teaching career developed, so did his tennis. He was awarded a tennis "blue" by the University of Melbourne in 1952 and captained the Combined University Tennis Team.

He enjoyed playing in country tournaments and won the Western Riverina Championships, played at Deniliquin, six years in a row from 1951 to 1956. He also conducted coaching clinics when he visited country centres for tournaments.

Geoff was also a regular participant in the Victorian Tennis Championships in the 1950s and, occasionally, in the Australian Championships where he played against some of the country's top players. He admitted losing to Rod Laver in the first round of the Victorian Championships in the late 1950s.

It was not unexpected that Geoff was appointed Caulfield's Firsts Tennis coach in 1949. In his 38 years as coach, his team won five Associated Grammar Schools of Victoria premierships in 1952, 1953, 1954, 1956 and 1957. The 1949 team was undefeated but the premiership was abandoned due to the polio scare. When Caulfield joined the Associated Public Schools, there was no official tennis premiership until 1987 but Caulfield won the "unofficial premiership" from 1961 to 1964 and in 1972. When the official premiership was introduced, Caulfield donated the premiership trophy, appropriately named the "R.G. Wilkinson Cup".

Although it is hard to imagine that Geoff had any "spare" time with all that teaching, tennis playing, coaching and administration, it is worth noting that he also coached the school's Second XVIII for 26 years and assisted with athletics coaching.

In 1979, when plans were getting under way for the

celebration of the school's centenary in 1981, Geoff was the logical choice for Secretary of the Centenary Committee. His long connexion with the school and his ability as an administrator made the work of the committee much more efficient than it could have been. As Centenary Co-ordinator, I could not overstate the value of the support Geoff gave to the Headmaster and to me throughout the whole exercise.

For many years, Caulfield managed to get by with just one tennis court although teams trained on courts in McWhae Avenue and at other local venues. Geoff oversaw the construction of four plexipave tennis courts at Caulfield Campus which were officially named the "R.G. Wilkinson Memorial Courts" after Geoff died.

On a number of occasions in the 1970s and 1980s, along with other members of the Dendy Park Tennis Club, Geoff played in the Australian Veterans' Team Championships. He was made an Honorary Life Member of Dendy Park Tennis Club in 1988 for service to the club.

Geoff retired from Caulfield Grammar School at the end of 1987 after an unbroken 45-year connexion with the school. After a fitting round of farewells, he was looking forward to a quieter life. Sadly, his retirement was foreshortened by ill health and he died on 6th October 1990, survived by his wife, Norma, and their two children.

ACKNOWLEDGEMENTS

The assistance of the following people in the preparation of this book is gratefully acknowledged:

Chris Adam; Dean Anderson; Dr Jeffrey Barnes; Jonathan Brett Young; Dr Ross Brooks, Jane Blunn; Martin Carlson, OAM; Melinda Clarke, The Friends School; Michael Collins Persse, OAM; Judith Gibson; Nick Ginsburg, Monash University; Tim Hughes, The Armidale School; Grace Jakes; Andrew Joseph, author of *My Malvern Grammar*; Vane Lindesay, author of *Noel Counihan Caricatures*; Edwin Lorkin; Jane Mayo-Carolan; Elizabeth Milford, author of *Anzac Surgeons of Gallipoli*; Rachel Muir; Juliet Nicolson, author of *The Great Silence*; Kay Owens; Jill Pennefather; Helen Pitt, author of *The House*; Lisa Polden, Devonport High School; Ian Pyman, AM; Tony Pyman; John Raven; His Honour Michael Rozenes, AO, QC; Paul Sheahan, AM; Brian Sidlo; John Silvester; Bernard Smith, author of *Noel Counihan artist and revolutionary*; Clarrie Stillman; Rear Admiral Rothesay Swan, AO, CBE; Greg Swinden, RAN History Unit; Gary Tyler; Vivien Whelpton; Dr Ian Wilkinson; and Peter Wilmot.

The Old School

www.ingramcontent.com/pod-product-compliance
Ingram Content Group UK Ltd.
Pitfield, Milton Keynes, MK11 3LW, UK
UKHW021327180426
11947UKWH00017B/1485